Forest Craft

A child's guide to whittling in the woodland

Richard Irvine

THANKS TO OUR MODELS: STAN, JAKE, KESI, MARIAMA, SCOTT, JOSIE, JAMES AND JOHAN. EXTRA THANKS TO STAN FOR DRAWING THE MAP ON THE CONTENTS PAGES AND CLAIRE FOR HER AMAZING HEADDRESSES!

First published 2019 by Guild of Master Craftsman Publications Ltd
Castle Place, 166 High Street, Lewes, East Sussex, BN7 1XU

Reprinted 2019, 2020, 2021, 2022, 2024

ISBN 978 1 78494 500 8

A catalogue record for this book is available from the British Library.

Publisher: Jonathan Bailey
Production: Jim Bulley
Commissioning & Senior Project Editor: Dominique Page
Editor: Honor Head
Managing Art Editor: Gilda Pacitti
Art Editor: Rebecca Mothersole
Illustrators: Sarah Skeate (cover), Rebecca Mothersole and Claire Owen (inside artworks), Ann Biggs (botanical drawings)
Photographers: Richard Irvine and Rebecca Mothersole

Colour origination by GMC Reprographics
Printed and bound in China

Picture credits:
Following backgrounds from Shutterstock.com: ninanaina – pages 1, 3, 4, 5, 15, 25, 32, 43, 44, 48, 51, 52, 55, 56, 58, 61, 62, 65, 66, 67, 70, 73, 74, 76, 79, 80, 82, 86, 89, 91, 92, 94, 95, 98, 101, 102, 104, 106, 109, 111, 112, 114, 117, 119, 121, 122, 125, 126, 128, 130, 132, 134, 137, 139, 140, 141, 142, 144, 146, 148, 150, 155, 156, 157; Creative Pixels – pages 11, 19, 22 29, 33, 52 (box), 108, 125 (box), 131, 155, 156. Elderberry leaves, page 84: photofriend/ Shutterstock.com.

FSC
www.fsc.org
MIX
Paper | Supporting responsible forestry
FSC® C020056

Foreword

As a Forest School Practitioner, Playworker and Trainer, one of the things that I have noticed is how absorbed people become when they are working with tools and wood. I think of working with wood as meditation with the hands: when it's going well, there is nothing that helps me get into a state of flow more than whittling. When the hands are busy, the mind can be free.

Children who might not naturally sit and focus on one task can find themselves completely engrossed, too. As a parent, it can feel risky to allow a child to use tools, but all the safety advice you need to adhere to can be found in this book. And the payoffs are extraordinary: some projects that may seem very simple to an adult require a great deal of perseverance for a child to complete, and in doing so, they build skills in resilience and patience. In addition, many of the projects extend well beyond the process of making, and encourage imaginative play that will not only educate but also keep children entertained for days.

I am so excited to see Richard sharing his ideas in this book – he has a wealth of knowledge that will benefit so many people, including Forest School teachers, families and other craftspeople. By delving into this book, you'll discover all the different techniques, hints and tips that Richard has practised and developed over the years, plus plenty of inspirational ways to put them to use. Armed with this information, you and the children in your care will be all set to have fun, experiment and follow your own creative paths.

Lily Horseman
Chair of the Forest School Association

For Suzie, Jake and Stan.

Contents

The projects

Introduction

I get a real buzz from all aspects of working with greenwood, and through this book, I hope to share this with you. Whether it's spending a few minutes making elder beads or passing a carefree hour crafting a whistle, while you're focused on your creation, time and the everyday stresses of life lose their hold on you. Then, when you've finished, you have the pride that comes from having made a beautiful thing using only the simplest of tools and the natural world around you.

As you walk through the woods searching for just the right branch, and learn to take advantage of its natural twists and turns, you're doing something that people have relied on and also enjoyed for millennia. By trying out whittling and carving you will discover so much about trees: their different woods and properties, and also learn which tools to use and how to care for them.

As a teacher and trainer, I've spent my career encouraging children, young people and adults to get outdoors and create things using simple hand tools. Through this book, my aim is to persuade more people to experience the delights of whittling outdoors in the woods. I believe it's one of the best ways to enrich the physical, social, emotional, creative and spiritual aspects of people's lives.

By working through this book, everyone can gain the basic skills they will need to enjoy crafting with wood and making things with their hands.

People often ask what age children can start using saws and knives, and the answer is always: 'it depends'. The ability to use a certain tool isn't necessarily related to age but rather to the development of motor skills, the capacity to focus and listen to instructions, and the strength to grip the tool and exert sufficient force. Often, our preconceptions about whether a child is ready or not can be overturned when we see what they can do when given the chance. It's important that children are supervised (ideally one-to-one) when starting out. The adult must pay close attention to the child's progress, mood and level of alertness, and be aware when it's time to take a break or save the next steps for another time.

All of the tools mentioned in this book should be used under close adult supervision.

How to use this book

This book begins with an introduction to the tools that will be used, how to care for them and how to use them safely. The range of tools needed is deliberately small in order to keep things cheap and simple. The section on which wood to use introduces some of the more useful trees and provides ideas on how best to source the right wood to work with.

The 20 projects that follow have been ordered so that the variety of tools and skills needed are introduced gradually, building up from simple sawing at the start to quite concentrated, fiddly whittling in later projects. It will be necessary to refer back to the techniques section for detailed instructions and safety advice when a new tool or way of working is introduced in a project. If you are new to working with wood in this way, or are introducing children to the craft, then it makes sense to start at the beginning and work through each project in succession.

The projects have been chosen for their novelty and fun, as well as for the range of techniques that are required to make them. A few of the projects included here are variations on well-known items, while others are my own ideas that you won't have seen before. Whether the objects have been made for centuries, or are more recent inventions, the individual maker can give them all a unique creative twist and interpretation. Woodcraft is therefore akin to storytelling, where good stories are passed on from person to person and changed or embellished by each successive teller. Of course, if you already have experience in working wood with hand tools, then you can dive in to any project, vary the instructions, employ your own techniques and carry on the creative tradition by making your own versions and adaptations.

As you start sawing, drilling, cleaving and whittling, there are a few key points to remember. First, the process is more important than the product. It's satisfying to successfully complete a project and have a functioning object to use or play with, but you'll find most of the joy and learning comes from the doing and improving. To that end, perseverance is vital. Don't give up when it doesn't go as well as you would have wished, and always take a rest away from the tools if you find yourself becoming tired or frustrated.

I suggest that you approach the projects with a sense of playfulness and never be afraid to experiment. Doodle; make stuff with no apparent purpose, just for the fun of trying. At worst you'll have some more firewood! To improve at anything takes practice – so practise! After 25 years of carving, I'm not an expert, but I do know that I continue to become more skilled with every project that I work on and enjoy this process immensely. So…. start the journey today: saw some firewood, sharpen a stick, make piles of chips and shavings, and start again when it doesn't work first time. But, above all, enjoy the age-old feeling of working with wood.

Before you start

Tools and equipment

All the projects in this book can be made using a very small number of basic hand tools and equipment. It's not necessary to spend a fortune when buying new tools but it does make sense to remember the old adage of 'buy cheap, buy twice'. If you're lucky, you may find a bargain tool that will do the job well and last a long time. I always keep my eyes peeled at my local recycling centre and at car boot sales and have found many great, if rather neglected, tools over the years.

Maintain the tools you have by keeping them out of contact with stones, soil and moisture. Dry your tools after use, apply a little mineral oil to prevent rust and lubricate any moving parts. Store in a safe, dry place that is well out of the reach of small children.

For cutting

A Bow saw

This particular saw lives in the boot of my car, ready and waiting for opportunistic wood harvesting. A decent bow saw will have a stiff frame and a way of tensioning the blade that is more than just either tight or loose. Frames that flex and blades that are not properly tensioned will make it extremely difficult to saw a straight, vertical cut. It's a good idea to get a saw with a moulded plastic handle that will protect your knuckles at the end of a cut. For pruning branches, an asymmetrical saw with a pointed nose will allow access to the tighter forks between a branch and the trunk. For two-person sawing with children, a symmetrical 'D'-shaped frame may be easier to use.

Blades generally have either a raker tooth pattern for freshly cut greenwood, or have peg teeth for dry wood. Don't worry too much about which blade your saw has; it is unlikely to make a noticeable difference for the small-diameter wood required for the projects in this book. What is much more important is that your saw blade is sharp. If sawing becomes too much effort, try replacing the blade – you may be pleasantly surprised by the result.

B Hacksaw

Hacksaws fitted with a blade designed to cut wood rather than metal can be used for small tasks, such as cutting elder beads (see page 44). Hacksaws usually come fitted with a very fine toothed blade designed to cut metal pipes. These easily clog up with wet wood fibres and become useless. It's important to fit your hacksaw with 'wood blades', which have much bigger teeth that do not fill with sawdust.

When fitting a new 'wood' blade to a junior hacksaw, make sure that the teeth are angled back towards the handle otherwise it will chatter and judder as you attempt to saw. Hacksaws with plastic moulded handles are gripped with the hand and wrist in a natural alignment and are easier for children to use than those with a tubular metal frame and handle.

C Pruning saw

A good pruning saw can be used instead of a bow saw for many tasks involving small-diameter wood. They are easy to carry and the blade folds into the handle, allowing it to fit into a coat or trouser pocket. All pruning saws should have a mechanism to lock the blade in position when sawing. Some also lock closed to prevent accidental opening. Pruning saws generally cut when pulled rather than pushed; however, some blades are ground to cut on the push and pull cut. It's important to know which type of saw you have to avoid bending the blade. A blade with fine teeth will make a cleaner cut, although it will take longer to saw through a larger branch.

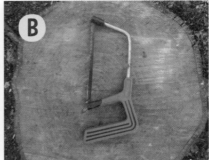

ⓓ Secateurs

These are nice to have for cutting twigs and branches under ¾in (2cm) diameter, but they are not essential. Good-quality secateurs can be taken apart for maintenance and sharpening.

ⓔ Sawhorse

Given the choice, I will always use a sawhorse when sawing wood. They can easily be made from scrap timber and a few screws. The addition of a couple of bolts means that the frame can fold and be transported in the boot of a small car or over a shoulder. The wide base creates a stable platform and long uprights from the legs make the ears of the horse, which will protect hands holding the wood should the saw jump out of the cut. Shorter lengths can safely be sawn using the horse.

Other options for holding your work

With an additional person to push the branch you are sawing, the wood you want to saw can be held firmly by levering it against two stems in a multi-stemmed tree.

A folding DIY workbench that can be used as a vice serves well if you're working on your own or with work that needs to be held tightly.

A log or stump can be used for cutting sections from longer lengths of wood. Placing the wood to be sawn over a fallen log or stump will raise it off the ground and help a saw cut open, as it will be under tension rather than compression. An additional person to hold the wood still is useful.

For carving

Knives

It's easy to be overwhelmed by the choice of knives available for carving wood. But the most important thing to remember when starting out is that the knife handle should fit your hand comfortably and that the blade should be sharp (see page 38). If this is the case, then I would strongly advise that you use a knife that you already own and learn how to use it safely.

In the brief guide below I've suggested a few points to consider if you are choosing a new knife:

Finger guards These are useful on knives for younger children – they stop hands from creeping down the handle and grasping the blade. As skills and confidence increase, the finger guards can get in the way of more intricate carving.

Blade shape Many children's knives have a rounded tip to prevent injuries. As skills progress to include finer carving, such as steep concave shapes, spirals and chip carving, a blade that tapers to a point will be essential.

Type of steel The knife blade may be made of carbon or stainless steel but, for the purposes of the projects in this book, it's not an important factor. To put it simply, stainless steel is

Knife with a single flat bevel, or a Scandinavian grind.

far more moisture resistant and less likely to rust. It is said to be more difficult to sharpen but it will hold its edge well. Carbon steel is easier to sharpen but more prone to corrosion by moisture, tannin in wood or acids from cutting fruit. I've always used affordable, Swedish-made, carbon-steel knives, which are widely available online.

Bevel grind This is a complicated topic, which is frequently debated and discussed by toolmakers and woodworkers the world over. For our purposes, it's advisable to look for a knife with a single flat bevel, which is sometimes called a Scandinavian grind. It's straightforward to sharpen, easy to control with the bevel in contact with the wood and suits the techniques described in this book.

Folding or fixed blade I still own and use my first knife: a French folder with a wooden handle and locking ring. Many households have a Swiss army knife or multi-tool and, if they're sharp, they may well be suitable for some of the projects that involve carving. Folding blades have the advantage of being easy to carry but the disadvantage of having a point of weakness in the hinge. This is a safety issue when using the knife to cleave or split wood (see page 34), and it's generally a very bad idea to use a folding knife in this way. Extra care is needed to avoid cutting your fingers when closing the blade. For these reasons I don't use folding knives with children and assume that you are using a fixed blade knife when making any of the projects.

Here are some examples of knives that are suitable for whittling and can be successfully used to make the projects in this book:

A **Sloyd** These short, fixed-blade knives taper to a sharp point, making them great for fine detail carving as well as everyday whittling. The wooden handles are large and comfortable to hold and can be customized to your own design by carving them down to size. The blade is made of laminated steel with the core made of harder steel, which is sandwiched between layers of softer steel. If you look carefully, you will see the transition on the bevel. This design is supposed to be more flexible and keep a good edge. Due to the softer steel on the sides, they are fairly easy to sharpen and generally are a joy to use.

B **Scout** This is similar to the Companion knife below but is made for smaller hands from thinner steel and is rounded off at the very tip to reduce the risk of puncture wounds. In my experience, the finger guards are really useful for younger children to stop their hands inadvertently creeping up the blade as they change their grip.

C **Companion** This is a general-purpose knife that is very versatile and can be used for many different tasks when spending time outdoors.

Tree stump

An old tree stump can be an invaluable base on which to carve and split wood. A clean old plank can also be used, or even an old breadboard or kitchen worktop for indoor winter carving.

It is important to note that penalties for breaches of the laws on knives can be serious. Before buying or carrying a knife outside of your own home it's advisable to be aware of the relevant local laws that apply. Please see Resources on page 158 for further information.

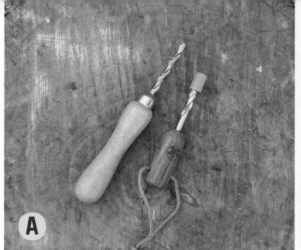

For drilling and removing pith

Ⓐ Palm drill

This is a general-purpose drill bit that is fitted and glued into a handle. Palm drills are small, cheap and easy to use but their range is limited to drilling a single size of hole. They can be purchased from Forest School equipment suppliers (see page 158) or you can make your own with a file handle, a general-purpose or wood drill bit and some 2-part epoxy glue.

Ⓑ Hand drill (egg-beater drill)

This is bulkier to carry than a palm drill but more versatile, as different-sized bits can be fitted in the chuck for making different-sized holes. My favourite drill is an old Stanley hand drill, which I purchased for a few pence at a car boot sale. It works as well as the day it left the factory over 50 years ago. Some models have an adjustable handle that can also be held as a pistol grip. Modern versions often have a 'plasticky feel', and are less robust than the older metal drills. It's important to use drill bits that are designed to cut wood rather than those for high-speed electric drills.

Ⓒ Drilling jig

This simple jig will wedge round sections of wood and grip them while drilling without the need for anyone's hands to be in the path of a descending drill bit.

Ⓓ Steel-wire tent peg

This item is used in projects that involve removing the pith from elder branches. A flat, rather than tapered, end is preferable to aid the removal of all the pith. Metal coat hangers or fencing wire can also be cut to size and fitted with a wooden handle, but require more care in use, as they tend to have sharp edges and to bend when pushing pith from long sections of elder.

Safety

First aid kit

Before you head off to find some wood and start crafting, grab a first aid kit, check the contents, including expiry dates, and make sure that you know what to do in case of cuts and puncture wounds. I make sure that I have plenty of plasters of different sizes, non-adhesive dressings, absorbent bandages and plenty of micropore tape and elastic bandages to hold dressings in place. Hopefully you'll never need to open it, but just make sure the kit is with you in case you ever do.

Should I wear gloves?

Whether you wear gloves when using tools is entirely a matter of individual choice. Giving children safety gloves can allow adults to feel more confident in letting them use sharp tools. However, good technique and thoughtful practice should protect both hands without the need for gloves. It's a bad idea to wear a glove on the hand that is holding a knife or saw, as your grip will be less firm and so you'll have less control over what you're doing. If you wish to wear a glove on the non-tool hand then it will need to be capable of resisting a cut from the tool you're using. Kevlar gloves (pictured below) will resist slicing and tearing but are little use against points of knives and drill bits, which will fit through the weave of the glove material. I might wear a glove on my non-tool hand to keep it warm when sawing wood during the winter months, but I never wear gloves when carving.

Which wood to use

The projects in this book require low volumes of small-diameter branch wood, which can usually be harvested by appropriate pruning or scavenging. You might be lucky enough to own woodland or have trees or hedges in your garden that you can prune. However, most of us don't and will need to look elsewhere for wood to saw, split, drill and whittle.

The UK has the lowest percentage of tree cover in Europe but there are still plenty of trees in local parks, hedges and woodlands. However, it must be emphasized that it is NOT okay to just go out with your saw and help yourself to growing branches or fallen dead wood. Always find out who owns or manages the land and ask permission. Other countries will have different rules, so find out about and follow local laws and customs when collecting wood.

It's a good idea to keep your eyes open for professional arborists (tree surgeons),

landscape gardeners and foresters going about their work in your neighbourhood. Asking politely for a bit of wood to pursue your hobby can lead to some interesting conversations about trees and carving, as well as a few branches that would otherwise be heading for the wood chipper.

If you have access to land in your garden, allotment, school or community where you might be able to plant some trees for the

future then, once established, a few hazel and elder bushes will yield a great deal of useful material that can be cut again and again without damaging the plants.

Some projects, such as the Frog Stick (see page 64), Whimmy Diddle (see page 70) and Feather Sticks (see page 92), can be completed using scrap wood, old pallets, commercial kindling and firewood.

Biosecurity

With several threats currently looming regarding tree health, such as acute oak decline and ash dieback, it's important to be aware that the bacterial and fungal pathogens that cause these conditions can be spread between woodlands via the mud on walkers' boots. Brushing and washing the mud from your footwear, bike and buggy wheels, etc. between visits to different woodlands can help prevent the spread of these threats to forest habitats.

Identifying trees and timber

Some projects will work best using the wood from a particular tree species. That means you will need to be able to correctly identify a range of trees in different seasons. There are lots of opportunities to learn about trees, such as by joining walks and courses organized by nature conservation groups like Wildlife Trusts; there are also mobile apps for phones and tablets as well as many good books to refer to. The Woodland Trust has a useful guide to help with the identification of UK trees (see page 158).

However, there is no substitute for direct experience within your local environment. The range and variety of species can be overwhelming to start with, so it might be worth just choosing one species at a time to focus on for a week or so. When out and about, ignore other trees and just pay attention to your species of the week. Notice where it likes to grow, the shape of the tree and its leaves or buds, patterns in the branches, bark colour and texture, and the patterns of any algae and lichens that live on it. Only read the relevant page of your tree ID book (or webpage) and try to find out some folklore or facts about the wildlife relating to your tree. A really comprehensive reference book is *Flora Britannica* by Richard Mabey.

The key to identifying the wood is to become familiar with its look, feel, smell and behaviour, which can really only be gained by sawing, splitting and carving it.

Finding material to work with is one of the joys of working with greenwood. It gives me a good excuse to go for a walk, encounter wildlife and notice all sorts of things that I would usually pass by.

The following eight tree species should get you started and are common in my local bioregion of south-west England and across much of the cool-temperate regions of northern and central Europe. Do not feel restricted to only using these or the species suggested in the instructions for each project. Experiment with whatever you are able to source and see how it works. Your own discoveries will be some of the most valuable woodworking knowledge that you will learn.

Tree species from left to right: cherry, elder, sweet chestnut, sycamore, hazel, alder, willow and ash.

Eight useful species

Elder (*Sambucus nigra*) Known as the 'Hag's tree', the elder is laden with folklore as well as fragrant flowers in late spring and dark berries in the autumn. The leaves, bark and wood are potentially mildly toxic and should not be burnt or eaten. However, I cannot find a single instance of any harm coming from just working with the wood. So, just be aware! Elder is really a shrub that does not tend to grow more than 10–13ft (3–4m) high. Its long, straight, vertical shoots, with two or three years' growth, are a mainstay of projects requiring a tube, such as the Duck Caller (see page 60) and Dart Gun (see page 146), as the soft, spongy pith can be easily removed without the need for a drill.

Some people say that it's wise to ask the hag's permission before cutting a branch, so listen carefully – silence indicates approval!

Notice the creamy wood colour, the wide white pith and the thick, corky bark with branch and leaf nodes.

Ash (*Fraxinus excelsior*) With its distinctive black buds, feathery compound leaves, mottled grey lichen-covered bark and easy-to-cleave wood, this is one of my favourite trees both to look at and to work with. In the Norse mythology of the Vikings, an ash tree called Yggdrasil is at the centre of the cosmos and is home to dragons and a meeting place of the gods.

Ash will usually split easily and is really useful for any projects where roundwood is split through the pith, such as when making Mini Furniture (see page 54), a Kazoo (see page 80), Feather Sticks (see page 92) and A Skulk of Foxes (see page 98). It can be difficult to carve convex curves and fine details, as its long fibres are prone to tear out. It has a low moisture content and dries quickly when split, meaning that you can collect up your cleavings to feed the campfire.

In the Norse mythology of the Vikings, an ash tree called Yggdrasil
is at the centre of the cosmos and is home to dragons
and a meeting place of the gods.

Sycamore (*Acer pseudoplatanus*) Sycamore is fairly easy to source, as it is often seen as an introduced invasive weed, especially by nature conservationists. As a member of the maple family, it has large, five-pointed leaves that open early in spring, casting dense shade on the woodland floor. This reduces light levels and the diversity of ground-cover plants. The tree itself supports few native invertebrates or birds compared with native tree species.

Sycamore is very forgiving to work with, feeling almost waxy under the knife. It's also great for kitchen items, as the wood imparts no taste to the food. I will happily cut as much wood as I need in a dense sycamore thicket without any feelings of remorse.

Willow (*Salix* species) Willows are common in wetlands and riverbanks across much of the world. They take root easily in damp ground and new suckers quickly sprout from pruning cuts. Some species will produce long straight stems valued by basket makers while others are more branched and brittle. They hybridize easily and different species of willow are sometimes hard to identify exactly. The bark contains the active ingredient salicylic acid, which has been used as a pain relief medicine for millennia and led to the development of the drug aspirin.

Willow is a great wood to start whittling with because it is the softest and easiest to work of the species in this list. It often does not split as cleanly as others but works well for those projects requiring roundwood, such as Fairytale Fungi (see page 86), Stick People (see page 120) and Gypsy Flowers (see page 132).

Willow is the perfect wood for making Gypsy Flowers.

Sweet Chestnut

(*Castanea sativa*) Technically another non-native tree, this was apparently introduced by the Romans for its food value. It is now naturalized and well established as a useful, commercially valuable tree, especially in the south-east of England. Sweet chestnut timber is very durable outdoors and is used for gates and fences, roof shingles and many other products. It cleaves beautifully with a satisfying ping, split pieces have a resonant ring when tapped, and it is really good for any noise-making projects like the Rhythm Sticks (see page 136).

Alder (*Alnus glutinosa*)

Like willow, this is a wetland and riverbank species that likes to keep its feet wet. It is easily identified from a distance in the spring as its buds give the canopy a hazy purple colour. Although the wood is not very dense, its high moisture content makes it hard work to saw because the sawdust sticks in the saw cut or kerf. Once sawn, the end grain changes to a distinctive orange colour. Alder is soft to carve and light once seasoned. In the past, it was used for clogs and pier pilings, and alder charcoal was ground up as an ingredient in gunpowder. If you are camping and forget your toothbrush, just peel the outer bark from an alder twig and brush your teeth with that instead.

Other tree species

I can also recommend looking out for birch, lime, rowan, field maple, aspen and poplar. I don't have access to these trees very often but I love to work with them when I can.

There are only a few trees that I would advise against at this stage; however, once you gain skill and experience, they are also worth using. So for now it might be best to avoid thorny trees, such as blackthorn and hawthorn; trees with very dense wood, like beech and hornbeam; and wood with gnarly grain found in species like elm and some oak.

Wild Cherry (*Prunus avium*)

Cherry is possibly the most visually interesting tree in this short list. Its display of white blossom makes it stand out in the woods in early spring. The dark reddish brown bark is marked by hundreds of long, horizontal lenticels (pores) and can sometimes peel around the trunk in curling sheets. The relatively hard wood has attractive, contrasting orange heartwood and creamy sapwood and, like other fruit woods, is enjoyable to carve.

Hazel (*Corylus avellana*)

Common, shrubby and multi-stemmed, this tree is a true woodsman's friend. When grown at sufficient density, it produces long, straight, flexible poles that can be cut again and again via the age-old, sustainable process of coppicing. The wood has a multitude of traditional uses in house building, woven fencing or hurdles, agricultural implements, bean poles, peas sticks, thatching spars and so on. It is very versatile and can be used in many of the projects in this book, especially small sculptural carvings and items requiring straight evenly tapered sticks, such as Feather Sticks (see page 92) and Gypsy Flowers (see page 132). It's nice to carve when green, it dries hard and mellows to a light nut-brown colour.

Three-cut pruning

Pruning a branch from a living tree can be a good way of harvesting craft materials, but it needs to be done sensitively and without harming the health of the whole tree. Most pruning of deciduous trees is best done when they are dormant through the winter. Some trees will leak lots of sap from a pruning cut, even if they are not in leaf, so it's wise to identify your tree and research it. The following method of pruning will do the least damage to the tree and give it the best chance of healing over the wound made by cutting. Before you start, check that you have permission to prune the tree and make sure that it's safe to do so.

1. First make an undercut about a third of the way through the branch, some way from where it meets the trunk.

2. Then make a cut from the top of the branch above the undercut but slightly offset away from the trunk.

3. Lastly, find the collar of bark where the branch joined the tree and make a finishing cut just on the branch side of it. Try to cut flush with the collar, not into it, as it contains the hormones that promote bark growth, which in time will cover over the wound.

Techniques

There are lots of safe ways to use the tools required for the projects in this book, and there are also a few that are unsafe. This brief guide is an introduction to get you started, rather than a fully comprehensive instruction manual.

Staying safe means being mindful of what you are doing and is often a matter of common sense. However, common sense is based on experience, so stick with the guidance below until you are practised and confident enough to improvise. If you discover a safe grip or cut that works for you, then feel free to use it. Just always ask yourself the 'what if?' question. What if things don't go as intended? Where will the tool end up? I often remember the words of John Rhyder, founder of the Woodcraft School in Sussex, who said 'If it feels dangerous then it probably is'.

When working with children, it's also really important to model appropriate handling of all tools in order to teach safe habits from the outset. There may be ways that we use tools ourselves that are not necessarily the way we would wish those in our care to use them! For that reason I make no apologies for going back to basics and stating what might seem blatantly obvious.

A

Sawing

A There are quite a lot of things to think about when sawing, from supporting and steadying the wood to how to stand, where to look, and how much force to use. The following is written with a bow saw in mind but the same principles apply when using a hacksaw or pruning saw. For pruning branches from a living tree, see page 29.

First, make sure that the wood you are sawing is held securely with your non-tool hand placed out of harm's way. If the saw blade jumps out of the cut, it is most likely to jump towards the centre line of your body. Keep the hand holding the wood behind the ears of the sawhorse or a good distance away from the saw cut.

Stand with your feet apart, in line with the saw, and with your dominant foot at the back.

Look down the frame of the saw and use the whole blade on each cut backwards and forwards.

Looking around the side of the saw to see where the cut is going will change the angle of the cut and make a straight cut less likely. If the blade bends in either the horizontal or vertical plane, it may stick but will at the very least rub against the side walls of the cut and be harder work. If the saw jams, do not apply extra force to move it: instead just stop, relax, reposition and try again, letting the saw, rather than your strength, do the work.

It may be tempting for young bystanders to try to catch a piece of wood as it falls to the ground. Make sure that they stand back and use a rope or branch to mark a safe distance if necessary.

Poking pith

B This may seem like stating the obvious but it is good to remind yourself to push the pith out of an elder branch with a tent peg in a way that the peg ends up somewhere safe rather than into you or someone else. Pushing through on to a soft surface, like the earth, will remove the pith and let the peg go through the bead and into the ground. If holding the work and the peg in your hands, pause to assess where the peg will end up before applying any force.

Drilling

C Palm drill
This simple tool still requires some strength and dexterity to control. Hold it in your dominant hand with the work sitting on a flat, stable surface, such as a tree stump. Drill a hole by pushing downwards while simultaneously twisting the drill in a clockwise direction. As with the tent peg, it's best to drill on to a surface rather than hold the work and the tool in your hands.

D Hand drill
Make sure that drill bits are firmly secured in the chuck by first hand-tightening it and then holding the chuck and rotating the handle. This tool uses a different range of physical motions from the palm drill. Downward pressure is still needed for the cutting edge of the bit to cut into the wood, but the rotation is created by winding the handle at the side. I use this as a two-person tool if the other user doesn't yet have the strength or dexterity to hold the drill steady at one angle and push down at the same time. Younger children may find it helpful to have an adult hold the top handle and control the downward pressure while the child turns the handle on the side.

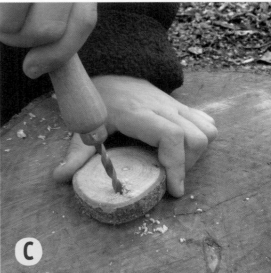

Carving

When carving with a knife, find a comfortable place to sit with enough room around you to be able to move freely without coming into contact with anyone else. Take care when removing the knife from the sheath. Hold the knife handle in one hand and push the sheath off with the thumb of the same hand. That way the knife stays still and the sheath is taken off in a controlled, safe manner.

It is also a good idea to get into the habit of placing the knife back in the sheath when you need to move around and never carry an unsheathed knife.

Always try to vary your sitting position and choice of knife grips regularly when carving, to look after your body and prevent aches and pains. Most people like to work to the same side of their body as their dominant hand but it can also be comfortable to lean forward with your forearms or elbows on your thighs.

There are lots of useful potential ways to grip the work and the knife. If you ever get into conversation with an avid whittler, spoon carver or bushcraft enthusiast, be prepared for an in-depth discussion of the pros and cons of each. The grips and cuts described below are those needed to complete the projects in this book and is by no means an exhaustive list.

Ⓐ Freehand carving

Sitting as described above, place the bevel of the knife on the wood, tilt it until you feel the edge bite and then move the knife forwards, removing a shaving of wood. Adjusting the angle and the force applied will determine how big a chip or shaving is carved. Always carve away from your holding hand. If you need to whittle in the other direction then turn the wood around rather than the knife. As you carve you may notice that it is easy to carve a clean surface in one direction but not the other way. I think of this as always carving 'downhill', away from the ends of the fibres of wood. If you carve 'uphill', the knife will dig into the ends of the fibres and stick or leave a messy, fibrous surface. With experience you will learn to read the grain of the wood and know which direction to carve in to get a clean surface.

Try to avoid:
- using the knife in a sawing motion. It should slice rather than tear through the wood.
- levering chips out at the end of a cut. Turn the wood and carve from the other direction or use a vertical stop cut to free wood that doesn't come away cleanly. Using the knife as a lever can fold and damage the cutting edge.

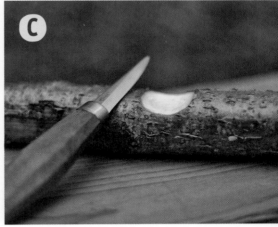

B Knee pull cut

Hold the knife handle in your dominant hand, with the cutting edge facing away from you. Line your thumb up along the handle and grip the other side with the tips of your fingers. Now place the back of the handle against the bottom of either kneecap and push it towards your leg. The knife will stay in this position and not move at all as the wood you are carving is pulled backwards in contact with the underside of the blade. Practise making a point on the end of a stick, first using big power cuts to remove lots of wood then reducing the force and making smaller and smaller shavings with long, fine, controlled cuts.

Never carve with the knife between your legs
The consequences of the knife cutting your upper leg and piercing the femoral artery are potentially life threatening. One wise young whittler I used to work with called this area between open knees and groin 'The Triangle of Doom'! She was not wrong.

C Concave cut

Making a concave cut with the knife requires changing the angle of the cut from steep to shallow as the knife moves through the wood. This is achieved by starting with the knife blade almost perpendicular to the wood and then rolling your wrist to change the angle of the cut so that it finishes almost parallel to the wood. This is used on the end section of a split stick to make the profile of a fox face in A Skulk of Foxes (see page 98) and to create the sweeping branches of the Tiny Pine Trees (see page 116).

D Batoning or cleaving

This is not so much a cut as a way of splitting the wood fibres apart. It is also the first of only two methods that involve pushing the knife into the end grain of a piece of wood. Always split on to another piece of wood and not the ground, stone, brick or concrete. Stand the round section of wood up on your stump and place the knife across the end section, making sure that it goes through the pith. Tap the back (spine) of the knife with a spare piece of wood (never metal on metal) to start a split then more firmly to split the section in two. Always line the knife up parallel with your body and think about where the arc of the knife will travel if it carries on through the wood and keeps moving. This technique can be hard on your knife, especially if you hit a knot in the wood. The choice of tool is important here. I never use a folding knife or the laminated steel Sloyd knife for batoning, I always prefer the more robust (and cheaper) general-purpose Companion.

E Vertical stop cut

Place the wood longways on a flat stump and put the blade of the knife perpendicular to it. Using the part of the blade closest to the handle will allow you to exert more pressure and make a deeper stop cut. Press down with the knife and roll the blade and wood to make an incised line around as much of the stick as you need to. This technique is often followed by the careful removal of wood on one side of the stop cut using the thumb push cut.

F Thumb push cut

This technique is a safe and trusty friend but if incorrectly or overused it can leave you with a sore and calloused thumb. The knife hand maintains the correct cutting angle and applies almost no force to this cut. All the pushing is done by the thumb of the hand that is holding the work piece. Try to keep the pushing thumb in contact with the handle rather than the metal spine of the knife.

G Power cut

This technique uses your upper body weight rather than the strength in your arm to either remove large chips or to make long curly shavings, such as in the Feather Sticks project (see page 92). Either stand at a waist-high chopping block or sit up on your knees by a low stump. Grip the knife as if you were holding the handlebars of a bike with your thumb wrapped around the handle, not on the spine of the blade. Place the bevel on the wood, adjust the angle to engage the cutting edge and then, keeping your knife arm straight, lean your upper body downwards to move the blade over the wood.

Make sure that your knuckles will pass by the edge of the stump and not impact the surface or graze the edge of the stump.

H Cutting towards your body

Apparently the Royal Marines say that you should always cut towards your mate. Intuitively this makes a lot of sense, as cutting towards your body would seem to be much riskier than carving away from yourself. There are, however, some safe techniques that can be used to achieve results that are not possible by only ever carving away from yourself. I reckon that at least half of my carving time employs these methods and the smaller and more fiddly your carving gets, the more useful they will become. Wait until you feel confident with all the other whittling techniques above before moving on to this.

The key to safe practice when cutting towards your body is to limit the potential travel of the knife by clamping your forearms against your lower ribs and only using the rotation of your wrist to move the knife. If you keep your arms like this, then the blade should not be able to come into contact with your clothes or body. Brace one end of the work against your body and keep your holding hand on the other end so that you are not cutting towards it. If you are wearing loose clothing, especially an expensive waterproof jacket, you might want to make a leather or wooden bib to protect your clothes from accidental nicks.

The following two cuts also involve cutting towards your body but with different grips on the work piece.

I Chamfer (apple peeling) cut

You can round off, or chamfer, a 90-degree edge using a series of thumb push cuts (see page 35). However, this technique allows you to get a single smooth surface rather than a series of flat facets. Hold the work securely in your holding hand and place the knife across the top of the work at the angle you want to cut. Don't try to remove too much wood at a time as you will need to use more force and therefore will have less knife control. First tuck your forearms into your lower ribs as described above. Brace the thumb of the knife hand below the cut and rotate the work with the holding hand so that the knife stays more or less still. Think about the potential follow-through of the knife, which should be limited by your wrist as well as the gap between the knife handle and crook of your thumb.

J Vertical slice cut

This is similar to the chamfer cut but instead of rounding a corner, we are using it to cut into the end grain to remove a chip from a thin (ideally less than $1/16$in/1mm) thick) flat section of wood and create a neat 'V' shape. Tuck your forearms into your lower ribs, again keeping your work and knife hand close to your body. Place the edge of the blade at 45 degrees to the wood and stretch the thumb of your knife hand as far as it will go down the piece of wood to act as a brace.

Slowly bring the knife into the wood while drawing the length of the blade across the wood. Use as little force as possible and stop the cut when you feel that the knife has travelled as far as it will. Remove the knife from the cut and keep the knife hand in the same position while you turn the work piece round 180 degrees. Aim this next cut to meet the bottom of the previous cut and remove a single triangular chip of wood. This technique is used in A Skulk of Foxes (see page 98).

Sharpening your knife

I come across many people who are worried that they will ruin their knife by sharpening it badly; however, if your knife is blunt it will be ineffective, hard to control, frustrating and tiring to use, as well as leaving a very poor finish on your work. There is no option but to bite the bullet and have a go – your knife will be no further use until you give it a sharp cutting edge again.

Learning how to sharpen your knife well takes practice until you develop an eye and the feel for a sharp edge. Repetition will build muscle memory and eventually sharpening can become a relaxing, even meditative thing to do. This is potentially a very technical subject, which can evoke strong opinions in many who have a preferred 'best' way of sharpening. Essentially it involves removing metal by abrasion from the whole bevel on both sides of the blade until a sharp cutting edge is regained.

I was taught to sharpen using Japanese water stones. These are man-made blocks of abrasive particles, which are used to sharpen metal blades by wearing away metal from the bevels of the tool. A grit number denotes the coarseness of the stone with smaller numbers, e.g. 250 grit, indicating coarser stones and larger numbers, e.g. 1,000 grit, indicating finer stones. Stones of 6,000+ grit can give a very sharp edge and a surface with a fine polish. Combination stones with 250 grit on one side and 1,000 grit on the other are available from good tool suppliers (see page 158).

To get you started, I have outlined the method I use below. This is very much a brief introduction and you may wish to learn more about sharpening and add further steps as you gain confidence. There are many other effective methods, some of which are signposted in the Resources section on page 158.

1. Soak the water stones before use but don't leave them in water over the winter if there is a risk of freezing, as they will crack.

2. Place your 1,000-grit stone on a flat, stable surface where you can sit or stand comfortably. A good light source is important, so you can see any tiny reflections from the edge of the knife.

3. Colour in the whole of the bevel with a black marker pen. As you work, you will be able to see any coloured areas of the blade that have not come into contact with the stone.

4. With the edge facing away from you, place the flat of the blade on the stone and then tilt it forward so that all of the bevel is in contact with the stone. You should see a bulge of water at the cutting edge.

5. Apply downward pressure on the bevel and push it away from you along the stone, making sure that you do not change the angle or let your fingers slide down in front of the edge.

6. Keep the knife at the same angle but release the pressure and slide it back towards you. To get the bevel of the belly and tip of the knife in contact with the stone, you will need to gently lift the knife handle as you push the blade along the stone. This is the trickiest part of sharpening and takes a good deal of practice.

7. Repeat the previous couple of steps eight to ten times. You should see grey water and streaks on the stone. These are tiny particles of metal worn away from the blade.

8. Turn the knife over so that the cutting edge is facing you. Start at the far end of the stone and repeat steps 4 to 7 in this direction to remove metal from the other bevel.

9. Carefully wipe the blade dry with a rag (away from, not towards the cutting edge), hold it up to the light and look at it from all angles. If you see a thin white line or patch of reflected light at the cutting edge then you have not removed enough metal and need to repeat the previous steps until you cannot see any reflection.

10. Put the knife back on the stone and make about 20 single passes on each bevel, as described in the previous steps (i.e towards the cutting edge), gradually reducing the downward pressure with each pass. This will help to remove any microscopic folds of metal, which have formed at the cutting edge.

Check the edge for reflections again and work on particular areas of the blade if necessary.

Strop your knife on a leather strop, old belt, cardboard box or flat board (e.g. MDF). You can add a fine abrasive to the strop, such as stropping compound or chrome polish. Toothpaste will also work as an improvised solution. Try to keep the bevel flat on the strop and push away from the cutting edge rather than towards it. Repeat this on alternate sides about 20 times.

11. Test the edge for sharpness by drawing it across a sheet of paper with a minimum of downward pressure. It should make a vertical slice without tearing the paper. I would strongly advise that you do not use your skin, hair or fingernails to test or show off how sharp the blade is.

The projects

Elder beads

There is something immensely satisfying about taking a hacksaw to a clean, finger-thick stick and sawing off a pocketful of beads, then popping out the pith of each one with a tent peg or 'pokey stick'. You can peel the 'beads' with a thumbnail in spring when the sap is rising and the bark just falls off, or carve patterns in the bark with a knife. The beads can be threaded on to a piece of leather cord, thong or coloured string to make necklaces or bracelets, or carved into little animals – they have even been used as 'currency' in a preschool mud-pie shop!

It is also a good idea to check the diameter of the pith. If it is narrower than a tent peg then try sawing a little bit off one end, as the diameter can be irregular within a single stem. Avoid using leaf and branch nodes as the pith often constricts at these points.

Apparently it's good manners when you prune an elder bush, to thank the 'Hags' or elder witches for the wood.

YOU WILL NEED:

- A branch of elder wood about ½–¾in (1–2cm) diameter
- Tent peg
- Junior hacksaw or secateurs
- Leather cord, thong or coloured string

1. Cut ½in (1cm) lengths from the end of the stick with a hacksaw. Holding the wood steady is crucial for safety and effectiveness. Elder branches are narrow and flexible, which means they'll bend when you're sawing. The branch needs to be secured close to the point of cutting, which potentially puts your holding hand at risk. I prefer to use a long-eared sawhorse to hold the wood (see page 17), so that the holding hand can be close to the saw cut but still protected by the ears of the horse. Alternatively, this can be a two-person job, with the stick sitting horizontally on a stump and the non-sawing person holding the wood still with their booted feet.

Make something with your beads! Cut appropriate lengths of leather thong, cord or coloured shoelaces and thread your beads to make necklaces or bracelets.

2. Use the tent peg to push the pith out from each section. Take care to ensure that the end of the tent peg is stopped by something other than your hand when it pokes through the pith. The safest way is to place the bead on the ground and push the tent peg through the pith into the soil.

3. Beads can be left plain with the bark on or decorated by peeling away all or some of the bark. Any carving with a knife is best done on the longer stick before sawing the lengths of bead.

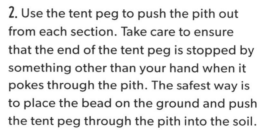

Little pot

Everyone needs containers to store important things. These simple little pots are perfect for keeping matches for firelighting, messages, wishes, salt or spices and anything else that might get lost or damp in your pockets or rucksack.

The lid of the pot is held in place by friction. The simplest lids can be made from the same piece of elder as the container, or it can be carved into a more elaborate shape from a different type of wood.

I usually just keep these pots in a coat or shirt pocket but an interesting variation is to make a pot that can be worn around the neck. In this case the lid is also held in place by the same cord that forms the necklace (see page 52). Instructions for this hanging version follow the making of the main pot.

There is lots of scope for decorating the pots with spirals, chip carving or paint (see page 156 for ideas).

YOU WILL NEED:

- A thumb-thick length of elder wood with a reasonable amount of pith – the bigger the better. There also needs to be a sufficient wall of wood around the pith that won't split while you are making the pot

- A dry, seasoned branch of any hardwood, such as hazel, with a diameter slightly larger than the pith of the elder

- Tent peg

- Sharp knife

- Fine-toothed pruning saw or hacksaw with a wood blade

For the necklace variation you will also need:

- A drill and 4mm or 5mm bit

- Cord or leather thong

1. Use the tent peg to poke the pith at least 4in (10cm) into the elder branch. Take your time and try to make the walls of the tube as clean and smooth as possible.

2. Cut about ½in (1cm) from the end of the tube. This will form the lid of the pot. Try to make this cut as straight as possible so that it will fit neatly back onto the container.

3. Plug the hole in the section you have just cut off with a tight-fitting length of dry, straight branch. It may take several tries to find a piece that is exactly the right size. Basket-making willow is ideal for this, as each length tapers and you can keep cutting bits off until you have found the size that fits. The plug should be flush with the top of the lid and protrude about ½in (1cm) on the other side to form the bung that will fit into the container.

4. Fit the lid and then cut the length of tube that will form the container from the rest of the branch.

5. Clean any remaining pith from the tube with the tent peg. If you remove the lid, it is important to remember which end it fits into.

6. Bung the base of the container with a tight-fitting length of the straight, dry branch. Insert it about ½in (1cm), then cut flush with the base.

7. You can leave the pot as it is, carve it to a shape or decorate.

Necklace variation

1. Use a palm drill to make a small-diameter hole through the base (tube and bung) perpendicular to the pot.

2. Drill another slightly larger hole through the lid, making sure both holes are aligned and parallel.

3. Cut 40in (1m) of cord and thread it through the hole in the base so that there is an even length on each side of the hole.

4. Thread the other ends of the cord through each side of the hole in the lid so that they pass each other.

5. Tie the ends together to make a necklace.

During one Forest School programme with a small group of preschool children, I put a small door between the buttress roots of a big oak tree. Once some of the children had discovered it they entered into some very involved small world play. They then asked to make some furniture for the fairies who they told me lived behind the door. I helped them use a saw and knife to make chairs and tables like those in this project and, as so often happens, they used all the offcuts and waste wood to invent new items to furnish the fairies' house.

Once you've made a table and a few chairs, why not use the same techniques to make a standard lamp, coffee table, sofa and a big flat-screen TV?

Mini furniture

YOU WILL NEED:

- *A straight, knot-free branch up to 3in (7cm) in diameter of any wood that will cleave easily, such as ash, sycamore, hazel, sweet chestnut, oak or willow (make life easy by avoiding beech, hornbeam, elm and any wood that is knotty or well seasoned)*
- *Another branch, a bit bigger than the last*
- *Pruning saw*
- *Sharp knife*
- *Stick or mallet*

Chair

1. Measure 3in (7cm) from the end of the smaller branch and saw about two-thirds of the way through.

2. Measure another ¾in (2cm) from the groove cut in the last step and saw right through the branch.

3. Stand the sawn branch on a stump with the groove closest to the stump.

4. Place the knife on the top of the branch and line it up with the base of the groove.

5. Gently tap the back of the knife blade into the branch with a stick or mallet until a section of wood is cleft away.

6. Repeat as many times as there are tiny people coming to dinner.

Table

1. Measure about ½in (1cm) from the end of the larger branch and saw a groove about ¾in (2cm) deep all the way around.

2. Measure about 1in (3cm) from the groove and saw all the way through the branch.

3. Place the sawn piece down with the groove closest to the stump.

4. Gently tap the back of the knife blade into the branch with a stick or mallet until a section of wood is cleft away. The split should stop at the grooved cut – be careful not to tap too hard or you will chop through the other side of the groove cut.

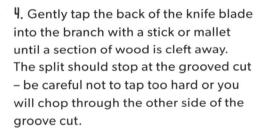

5. Turn the piece of wood less than 90 degrees and repeat step 4 until you have gone all the way around.

6. Repeat step 5, splitting smaller sections of wood each time to leave a round table leg.

7. Turn the wood over and you have made a micro round table.

QUACK QUACK

QUACK QUACK

Duck caller

Wildfowlers who hunt water birds often use duck calls to lure the birds towards their hide. There is a huge range of commercial callers which, in the hands of a skilled user, can imitate up to eight different duck sounds. It's unlikely that the simple device in this project will fool a mallard, but it does sound like a duck quacking and is likely to at least raise eyebrows and induce spontaneous laughter!

YOU WILL NEED:

- A knot/node-free length of freshly cut elder, about ¾in (2cm) in diameter and 4in (10cm) long
- Pruning saw
- Tent peg
- Sharp knife
- Thin card
- Sticky tape
- Pen or pencil
- Scissors

PUT YOUR MOUTH OVER THE END OF THE DUCK CALLER AND BLOW!

1. Use the tent peg to push the pith all the way through the elder branch. Make sure all of the pith is removed and the tube is as clean and smooth as possible.

2. Use a knife to whittle one end of the tube to a 45-degree angle.

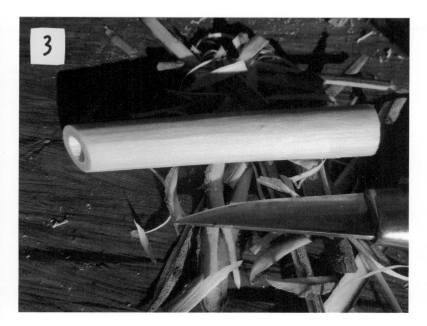

3. Peel off the bark and leave the tube to dry in the sun and wind for an hour or so, until it no longer feels damp.

4. Place the angled end of the tube on some thin card and carefully draw around it with a pen or pencil. Extend this outline by drawing a rectangular tab – this will be used to attach the card to the elder tube.

5. Cover the drawn outline with clear tape. Cut around the outline and fold a hinge in the card where the tab meets the outline of the end of the tube.

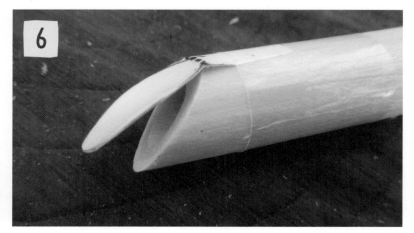

6. Tape the tab tightly to the elder tube so that the hinge lines up with the edge of the angled end. Then fold the flap of card at the hinge so that it almost completely covers the end of the tube.

This is another instrument for the woodland samba band (see Elder Whistle, page 74, Kazoo, page 80, and Rhythm Sticks, page 136). This is similar to the Latin American percussion instrument called a *güiro*. I call it a frog stick because it sounds a bit like a croaking frog when a striking stick is rubbed along the ridges of the instrument. Once you've mastered this basic version, there is huge scope for experimentation. Try changing the notches to a different pattern or adding more teeth in the same space. Have a go with different types of wood and different sizes, and then get creative with rhythms. Can you play the cha-cha-cha?

Frog stick

YOU WILL NEED:

- *A straight hardwood branch, such as hazel or sycamore, about 15in (40cm) long and ¾–1in (2–3cm) in diameter*

- *A smaller-diameter hardwood stick of a similar length*

- *Hacksaw fitted with a wood blade*

- *Sharp knife*

1. Saw a series of parallel notches about ¾in (2cm) apart and ½in (1cm) deep along the middle section of the larger stick. Leave 4in (10cm) untouched at either end. You will need the ends free to hold on to when you start whittling the notches.

2. Place the blade of the knife halfway between two of the vertical cuts and carve down towards the base of the next vertical notch. Use the thumb push cut (see page 35) to carefully control where the knife stops. Repeat this process all the way along the stick.

3. Turn the stick around in your hand and work in the other direction to repeat step 2.

4. The end result will be a series of peaks and valleys. You can saw off the uncarved wood from one end of the stick if you wish.

5. Carve two slices from the smaller stick to make a sharp edge, which will rub over the ridges in the bigger stick.

Take the smaller stick and rub it quickly over the notches to make a croaking noise. Try out different diameters and types of wood for the scraper to find the optimum noise maker.

FROG STICK

Whimmy diddle

This oddly named object is a traditional American folk toy, sometimes also called a Gee-haw Whimmy Diddle, a Hooey Stick or Whammy Doodle. By rubbing the thin stick over the ridges the propeller will spin around. The magic happens when the operator yells 'Gee! Haw!' or 'Hooey!' and then, mysteriously, the propeller starts to spin in the other direction. There isn't really any magic involved but there is quite a bit of physics, which is nicely summarized by this equation:

$$F_x(t) = X\cos(wt + \emptyset)$$

I don't understand it either! But the main aim is to make it work and astound your admiring audience. The trick is revealed in the last step of the instructions. Once you've made a Frog Stick (see page 64), it's easy to convert it into a Whimmy Diddle with the addition of a propeller at one end of the stick. You may also need to add some more ridges towards the propeller end. The instructions begin with a ready-made Frog Stick.

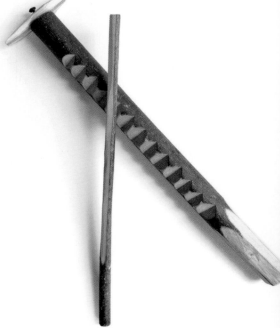

1. Baton (see page 34) the 2in (5cm) long stick twice with the knife to split out a rectangular section about ⅛in (2–3mm) thick.

2. Shape the sliver to a propeller shape if desired. This is not essential for the toy to work but it looks better. The propeller should be roughly symmetrical and evenly weighted on each side.

3. Use the tip of the knife in a circular motion to make a hole in the centre of the propeller that is about twice the diameter of the nail. Test that the propeller spins freely.

4. Put the nail through the hole in the propeller and push or hammer it into the centre of one end of the Frog Stick.

Hold the Whimmy Diddle and the small stick as shown. Rub the small stick over the ridges and watch the propeller spin. Making it change direction takes practice but can be done surreptitiously by pressing the index finger of the hand holding the small stick against the body of the Whimmy Diddle.

Elder whistle

This may well qualify as the classic elder woodcraft item. It's super simple but takes some practice to be able to make it reliably. I imagine that once upon a time, in a romantic golden age, when every child roamed the woods and meadows with their pen knives, the air was filled with the shrill, piercing sounds of elder whistles.

Taking time over the first step in making the whistle is critical; it's really important that you push the pith about 4in (10cm) into the stick but not all the way through. The bore of the tube must be burnished smooth and be completely free of bits of pith, i.e. 'as clean as a whistle'. Every face and edge should be free from wood fluff, pith and other 'hairy bits' so that there is no impediment to the flow of air that would otherwise make a breathy whistle or no noise at all. In my experience, a stick with a bigger diameter of pith is easier to make work, and also makes a deeper noise.

YOU WILL NEED:

- A knot/node-free length of freshly cut elder about ¾–1in (2–3cm) in diameter and 4–5in (10–12cm) long
- Pruning saw
- Tent peg
- Sharp knife

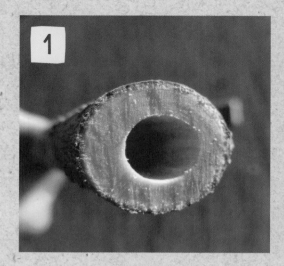

1. Push the tent peg about 3–4in (8–10cm) into the pith but not all the way through. Use the edges of the end of the peg to scrape all of the pith from the side walls of the tube. Spend some time on this to make sure that the walls are totally pith-free, then use the side of the tent peg to burnish the inside of the tube until it's smooth.

2. Make a vertical stop cut (see page 35) with the knife about ¾in (2cm) from the hollow end of the stick.

3. Use the knife to make a thumb push cut (see page 35) towards the vertical cut. Be careful not to cut too far or you will cut all the way to the end of the whistle.

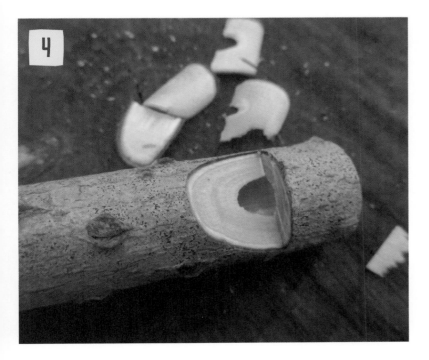

4. Repeat this combination of thumb push and vertical cuts until a 'D' shaped hole is made into the hollow part of the whistle. This hole is called the window. Make sure that there are no rough edges or stringy fibres in the hole as that will interfere with the smooth flow of air required to make the whistling sound.

5. Cut a 2¼in (6cm) dry, straight branch that is marginally bigger than the diameter of the hole in the body of the whistle. Whittle off the bark if necessary. Check that it will fit tightly inside the hole.

6. Use the knife to carve small shavings along the small stick until it has a 'D' shaped profile. More than half of the profile should remain. Again it's really important that this is smooth and no fibres are sticking up to impede the flow of air. This piece is called the fipple plug and will leave a gap or 'windway' for air to flow into the whistle where it will hit the sharp edge or 'lip' of the window.

7. Insert the fipple plug into the hole at the end of the whistle until it is flush with the vertical wall of the window. Looking closely at the end of the whistle, you should be able to see through the windway.

8. Put the fipple end of the whistle to your lips and blow firmly. If it makes a noise, then you can cheer and give yourself a pat on the back. Now skip straight to step 9. If the noise was absent or weak and breathy, it is time to tweak the fipple. It is important to only make very small adjustments and re-test the whistle after each change. First try twisting the plug so that the windway lines up with the sharp edge of the window. Then try moving the plug small amounts in or out of the hole. Finally, remove the plug and shave small slivers of wood from the flat surface of the plug to increase the size of the windway.

9. You may have to fiddle with your mouthpiece (known as a fipple) for some time but eventually you WILL get it to make a noise. Patience and persistence are key! When you are happy with the sound that your whistle makes, trim the plug flush with the mouthpiece.

10. For a recorder-style mouthpiece, whittle a concave section from the body of the whistle under the fipple plug.

AS THE WOOD DRIES, IT WILL SHRINK AND CLAMP TIGHT TO THE ALREADY DRY FIPPLE PLUG. THIS IS LIKELY TO CHANGE THE TONE THAT THE WHISTLE MAKES OR EVEN STOP IT MAKING A NOISE ANY MORE. THINK OF THAT AS AN OPPORTUNITY TO GO OUT AND MAKE ANOTHER ONE!

The kazoo is another amusing noise maker which uses the principle of a vibrating 'reed' to generate a buzzing noise over whatever you say, sing or hum through it. A version of this device is also used to make a sound like a rabbit in distress to attract larger predator animals like foxes or coyotes into view. I prefer to use the kazoo as a musical instrument in a woodland samba band or just as a comic voice distortion device. With several of these in the hands of a group of children it's possible to make perhaps the most annoying noise in the world. Be warned!

Kazoo

WHY NOT TRY USING A LEAF AS A REED? YOU COULD EXPERIMENT WITH WHATEVER YOU FIND IN THE WOODLAND. YOU COULD EVEN USE PART OF YOUR HAT!

ZZZZZZZZZZZZZZZ!!!!!!!!!!

ZZZZZZZZZZZZZZZ!

ZZZZZZZZZZZZZZZ

YOU WILL NEED:

- A 6–8in (15–20cm) length of straight, knot-free branch, about 1–1½in (3–4cm) in diameter – choose a wood species such as sycamore or ash, which is likely to split cleanly through the pith
- Sharp knife (or hacksaw for younger children)
- Pen or pencil
- String or elastic bands

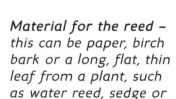

Material for the reed – this can be paper, birch bark or a long, flat, thin leaf from a plant, such as water reed, sedge or palm tree.

A hacksaw can be better for younger children to use when making the stop cuts instead of using the knife.

1. Split the branch in half lengthways by batoning (see page 34) with the knife.

2. Use the pen or pencil to shade in a space about 3in (8cm) long on the flat surface in the middle of each half of the branch. These should match exactly when the two halves are put together again.

3. Make a ¹⁄₁₆in (2mm) deep stop cut at each end of this space using the hacksaw or vertical push cuts (see page 34) with the knife. Repeat for the other side of the split branch.

4. Carve from the middle of the space towards a stop cut to remove the wood from the shaded space. Turn the wood and carve towards the other stop cut. Repeat for the other half of the branch.

5. When put back together, this will make a narrow rectangular window through the wood.

6. Place the reed between the two halves of wood and fasten together tightly at one end with string or elastic bands.

7. Pull the other end of the reed tight and clamp it in position between the two halves of wood before fastening this end tightly, as in step 6. Alternatively, leave the reed overlong and make the second fastening quite loose. You can then pull on the reed to vary the tension as you blow and make more varied noises.

EXPERIMENT WITH NOISES BY PULLING ON THE REED.

Fairytale fungi

Fungi are a fascinating group of organisms. Many are useful to us as medicines, for making bread and cheese, in fermentation and as a food in themselves. Mushrooms are the fruiting bodies of fungi, which mostly exist out of sight as tiny threads called mycelium. These are an essential part of woodland ecosystems, helping to break down dead wood and leaves, releasing their nutrients back into the soil. Some mushrooms are also toxic to humans so it's a good idea not to touch or pick any that you're not totally sure you've identified correctly. There is something wondrous about finding fungi on an autumnal walk in the woods or fields. This project starts with a basic fairytale fungus, but you can do some research and try to create other mushroom shapes or even try and carve a particular species.

YOU WILL NEED:

- *A straight, knot-free, 15½in (40cm) long branch of 1½in–2in (4–5cm) diameter – willow, sycamore, hazel and ash are all ideal for this project*
- *Sharp knife*
- *Pruning saw*

1. About 2in (5cm) from one end, saw a groove about ½in (1cm) deep all the way around the branch. This will define the transition between the cap and stem of the mushroom.

2. Measure another 2in (5cm) from the groove and saw the whole piece from the branch.

3. With the cap of the mushroom facing downwards, place the knife across the sawn section of wood about ½in (1cm) from the edge and gently baton (see page 34) the back of the knife with the leftover piece of branch.

4. Turn the wood a little and repeat this process about six times until you have something that looks like a small mallet.

5. Keep the wood in the same position and carve downwards to shape the stem. You can hold the top of the stem with your thumb and start the carving cuts at least ½in (1cm) below where you are holding.

6. Any shavings that stay attached to the branch can be freed with vertical cuts with the knife.

7. Shape the cap of the mushroom to a dome or a point by carving down towards the work surface.

Carving convex shapes

To give the mushroom a realistic, organic shape, you will need to add curves to the stem and cap.

Once the knife has bitten into the wood you can gently roll your wrist away from your body while carving downwards to make a concave shape in the stem. It's important that each cut stops when it is parallel to the grain of the wood. It's useful to think of carving as always being 'downhill'. If you try and carve 'uphill' into the grain, then the knife will stick and you will end up with a jagged rather than a smooth surface.

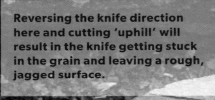

Reversing the knife direction here and cutting 'uphill' will result in the knife getting stuck in the grain and leaving a rough, jagged surface.

The knife must cut 'downhill' towards the end of the work, or the bottom of a concave 'U' shape, as shown here.

The lines show the wood fibres and orientation of the grain.

To carve any shape resembling a 'U', it will be necessary to turn the work and carve in the other direction towards the bottom of the 'U'.

Feather sticks

This project is a crossover into the world of 'bushcraft' (otherwise known as pottering around the woods and making yourself comfortable with your skills and knowledge of things you can find around you). Feather sticks are made as a reliable way of lighting a fire in a winter refuge or woodland camp. When small twigs are too wet to use as kindling, we can make feathersticks and turn large-diameter branchwood into easy-to-use firelighters. By splitting and carving, we can create the tinder and kindling needed to ignite bigger pieces of fuel using just one match, or, with a lot of practice, even a spark from a fire striker.

Apart from being a very useful thing to be able to make, it's included in this list of projects as it's a really good way of developing the skill of controlled straight-arm carving. It will take some practice to consistently shave long ribbons of wood down to a single point without cutting them from the stick but is worth the effort of repetition. The skill is transferable to many whittling projects, such as the Magic Elder Wand (see page 110) and Gypsy Flowers (see page 132).

YOU WILL NEED:

- Rather than the freshly cut greenwood used for most other projects, use a length of seasoned, dry wood that has not started to decay and go crumbly or 'punky'. Start with something about 2in (5cm) in diameter and 8in (20cm) long, avoiding knots if possible. Shop-bought kindling is also good to practise on
- Pruning saw
- Sharp knife

1. Baton (see page 34) the knife to split the wood through the pith into six or eight equal wedge-shaped sections.

2. Choose one section to work on and carve away the pith from the full length to leave a flat surface where the pith was.

3. Find a place where you can carve onto a stump or chopping block with your arm fully extended. I kneel on the ground with my upper legs straight and carve with a straight arm onto a stump on my right-hand side. This technique uses the weight of your upper body to do the work rather than muscles in your arm flexing your elbow. The carving action is a slight leaning motion towards the knife arm side of your body. Place the knife at 45 degrees to one side of the flat surface carved in step 2, find the bite point of the knife where it will just cut into the wood then gently lean your body into the cut and follow the shaving down to about 1½in (4cm) from the end of the stick.

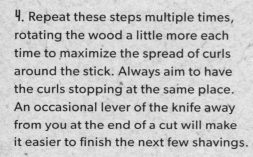

4. Repeat these steps multiple times, rotating the wood a little more each time to maximize the spread of curls around the stick. Always aim to have the curls stopping at the same place. An occasional lever of the knife away from you at the end of a cut will make it easier to finish the next few shavings.

5. Rotate the stick to the other side of the flat surface made in step 2 and repeat step 3. You should now have two ribbons of curled wood still attached to the stick at roughly the same point.

6. As the stick gets thinner, carve more slowly and reduce the pressure on each cut to make finer shavings that form tight curls. When you've made a good bunch of curls and the stem of wood behind them is starting to feel fragile, it's time to stop!

7. A minimum of four feather sticks should be enough to create the core of a fire, to which you can add other small split kindling.

A skulk of foxes

Did you know that the collective noun for several foxes is a 'skulk'? This intriguing wood doodle appeared online a few years ago and has become a popular project using a few basic cuts but some slightly trickier grips. Many other animals with ears and a nose can be carved in this same way, using a photo as a reference to help you make adjustments to the skulk instructions for shape and proportion. I find that making a whole set or skulk is a good way of developing technique, consistency and also memorizing the sequence of procedures. Once I've split the wood into six or eight sections, I repeat each step of the instructions on each blank before moving on to the next step and repeating it. Some people find that this sort of 'production whittling' defeats the object of carving to relax but I find the simple repetition quite meditative.

YOU WILL NEED:

- A straight, knot-free, 8in (20cm) length of easy-to-cleave hardwood about 2¼in (6cm) in diameter – wood such as ash, chestnut and cherry all work well

- A length of thick string to tie around the wood

- Saw

- Sharp knife

- Black pen or paints for decoration

1. Tie a length of string around one end of the branch to secure the piece in place.

2. Baton the knife to cleave the branch into four, six or eight equal sections (see page 34). Make sure that the knife is always placed across the pith of the wood to maintain control and prevent the split 'running out'.

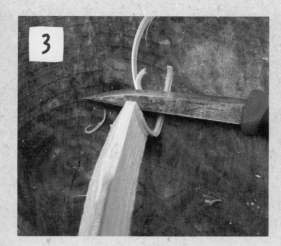

3. Remove the string and choose one section of wood to work on. Carve away the pith at the pointed edge to make it flat.

4. Make a firm vertical stop cut (see page 34) all the way around the section about 1½–2in (4–5cm) from the end. This line will define the head and neck of the fox.

5. Use a thumb push cut (see page 35) to remove wood from the neck of the fox up to the vertical stop cut. As more wood is removed, you will need to repeat the vertical stop cuts to free the shavings. Rolling your wrist while making the thumb push cuts will give the neck a slightly concave profile.

6. Create a chin for your fox by carving a 45-degree bevel from the head towards the top of the neck. Remember not to carve towards your holding hand.

7. Define the nose and face by making concave cuts (see page 33) towards the end of the stick, starting about ½in (1cm) above the neck. Thin the very top with some cuts on the bark side. The thinner this is, the easier it will be to shape the ears.

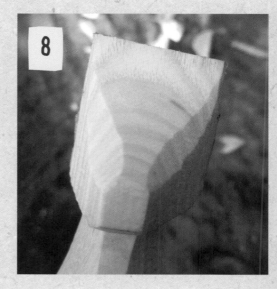

8. Use a sweeping thumb push cut to add a 45-degree bevel to each side of the face and the back of the head.

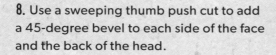

9. To define the ears, you will need to remove a triangular wedge from the thin section at the top of the head. Place the knife at an angle across the top of the head and make a vertical slice cut (see page 37) at an angle into the grain. Turn the wood around and repeat in the opposite direction, making sure that both cuts meet at the base of the ears. Tidy up the outside edge of each ear to bring them to a point.

WARNING: TAKE GREAT CARE WITH THIS WHOLE STEP. THINK CAREFULLY ABOUT HOW YOU ARE HOLDING THE WOOD AND ASK YOURSELF WHERE THE KNIFE WILL END UP IF THE CUT IS NOT AS CONTROLLED AS YOU INTEND. PAY SPECIAL ATTENTION TO YOUR HOLDING HAND AND THE THUMB OF YOUR KNIFE HAND.

10. Decorate your fox face with eyes, ears and nose in simple black pen or grab the paints and get creative.

11. Repeat for the other sections of wood that you split from the branch and put all the foxes back together like a jigsaw.

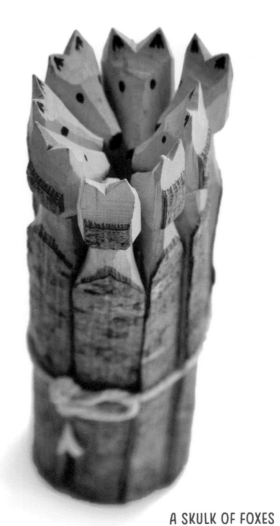

This clever design uses the top circle of branches and stem of a spruce or fir tree and is an ideal project for early January when it's easy to find discarded Christmas trees. It is especially satisfying to make a useful product from something that would otherwise just be burnt or turned into woodchip. If trees are collected locally for recycling, you may be able to harvest a supply of materials and make several whisks for friends and family. You could also then experiment with your own variations on this technique and design.

Spruce tree whisks are probably as old as humankind and are still sometimes used in northern and central Europe where conifer trees are common and folk crafts and traditions are still practised. Large versions of these were traditionally used in Swiss cheese-making to cut the curds. Sometimes the branches are bound to the handle using string or a binding made from split roots or inner bark, but this makes it difficult to clean properly after use so I prefer this unbound design.

Whisk

YOU WILL NEED:

- The top 24–40in (60–100cm) of an already felled spruce or fir tree
- Saw or secateurs
- Sharp knife
- String
- Saucepan (ideally stainless steel with lid)
- Heat source: kitchen hob, camping stove or open fire
- Heatproof gloves
- Old mug
- Fine sandpaper and food-safe oil (optional)

1. Cut the stem to include the top circle of branches and around 12in (30cm) of stem for the handle.

2. Remove any lower branches that are not going to be part of the whisk.

3. Decide which way up the whisk will be. Bending the branches backwards towards the stem will give a larger diameter piece of wood to use as the handle. Cut off the stem on the other side of the branches, leaving about a couple of inches (a few centimetres) to carve to a point.

4. Peel all the bark off. Scraping the needles off first with the back of a knife will make it easier to see what you are doing. Peeling is really easy in spring but it's a sticky, fiddly job in January. Try not to cut into the wood and don't worry if you don't get all the bark off at this stage.

5. You can leave the handle as it is or carve it to a shape that you like. Carving a bulge at the top and an octagonal section handle will make it easy to twirl between the palms of your hands. Carve the stub of stem left below the whorl to a point to make it easier to spin on the base of the pan.

6. If possible, bend the branches back towards the handle and bind them with string to form the balloon of the whisk. If this isn't possible, then jump to step 7. It's wise to bend the branches gently at this point and not use too much force or the wood may crack or snap. You will be able to increase the bend and play with the shape once the wood has been boiled.

Norwegians would have called your whisk a *turru*.

7. Put the whisk in a stainless steel pan of boiling water with the lid on if possible. Let it simmer for at least 10 minutes. The water might turn pink and smell like pine shower gel!

8. Using heatproof gloves, remove the whisk from the hot water and pull the ends of the branches up through the string to bend them to shape. At this point it should be easy to scrape any remaining inner bark from the branches using the back of a knife or even a thumbnail.

9. Continue with this process if you wish to adjust the shape of the whisk. Place the whisk balloon down into a mug. This will help to shape the hot wood. Leave it until the wood is cool and dry.

10. Remove the string and trim the branches to an even length. Keep the balloon shape or go for traditional shorter stubs. It can now be sanded smooth and treated with a food-safe oil or just used as is, untreated.

11. Make some hot chocolate with milk and good-quality dark chocolate using the whisk to mix the liquid. The bent branches may open out in the hot milk but usually return to the shape achieved in step 10 once cool and dry.

Bending wood

Wood is made of cellulose fibres (used to make the paper in this book) and a compound called lignin, which gives wood and bark its rigidity. Lignin becomes soft when heated to above 212°F (100°C), which allows the wood to be bent without breaking the cellulose fibres. When the wood cools and dries, the lignin hardens again and the wood retains its new shape. Large pieces of wood used for making furniture are usually bent around a pre-made jig after being heated with steam in a steam box or plastic bag. Small pieces of wood can be boiled in a pan of water until pliable and then bent into shape until dry and cold. Make sure that you avoid scalding your hands by using oven gloves or welder's mitts when handling the wood straight out of the pan or steam box.

WARNING: AVOID SCALDING YOUR HANDS BY USING OVEN GLOVES OR WELDER'S MITTS WHEN HANDLING THE WOOD STRAIGHT OUT OF THE PAN OR STEAM BOX.

Magic elder wand

> *'The truth is that only a highly unusual person will find their perfect match in elder, and on the rare occasion when such a pairing occurs, I take it as certain that the witch or wizard in question is marked out for a special destiny.'*
> *Wand Woods*, J.K. Rowling,
> Pottermore Wizarding World

It is said that the wand chooses the wizard and that only a very special wizard will be able to master the elder wand. Try this if you dare, but be careful to make sure that your wand does not backfire! You can make up your own spell for your wand but I like to use the spell that comes with each species of wood in its scientific, or binomial, Latin name. For the elder wand, this is *Sambucus nigra*. This is a good way to learn a bit more about tree species and their individual properties as you choose and work with different types of wood.

Great wands can be made from any type of wood, but I quite like to use resinous pines and branches dropped by oak trees in the winter. This project is an exercise in freestyle carving and, whatever wood chooses you, you can whittle away to make it your own. The instructions are for a basic elder wand, which is especially fun to make as you can easily give it a magical core of your choice.

YOU WILL NEED:

- An elder branch, about 12–16in (30–40cm) long and ¾–1½in (2–4cm) in diameter, with as few leaf and branch nodes as possible

- A smaller diameter straight, dry twig

- Tent peg

- Saw

- Sharp knife

- Pen and paper

- Oil for finishing (see page 155)

- Magical materials for the core

1. Push the tent peg into the soft pith at the handle end of the elder branch and work the peg until you've made a smooth tube about 2in (5cm) deep. This will be the core of your wand and we will return to it in the final steps of the project.

2. Make another similar hole at the tip end of the stick and plug it completely with a tight-fitting, straight, dry twig.

3. Taper the wand from the handle to the tip. It is easiest to start by carving four faces so that the tip of the wand has a square section. Leaving the bark on part or all of the handle or grip of the wand gives an interesting effect. This is best done in the autumn or winter, as the bark may well just slip off in spring-cut wood.

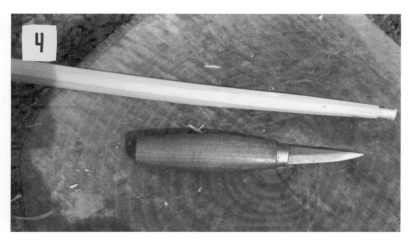

4. Remove the corners from your square section so that the length of the wand has eight faces, then continue carving off the corners using long, controlled knee pull cuts (see page 33) until the surface feels fairly smooth.

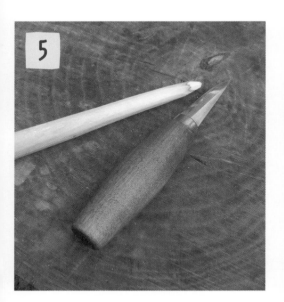

5. Round off the tip of the wand by carving at a steeper angle. This will involve also cutting through the plug inserted in step 2.

6. Remove sharp edges and shape the handle end so that it fits comfortably in your hand.

7. Now decorate your wand with spirals. Place the wand on a flat stump, put the knife across the length at 45 degrees and roll the knife and wood to make a vertical cut that spirals around the length of the wood.

8. Use a thumb push cut (see page 35) to carefully remove chips from the handle side towards the vertical stop cut. This will accentuate the spirals and make the pattern three-dimensional.

9. For an optional interesting effect, start another vertical cut directly opposite the start of the first cut, rolling wood and knife as before and keeping an equal distance between the spirals as you move up the wand. Repeat the thumb push cuts as in step 8.

10. Keep whittling until you have a shape that you like. Remember that you can't add wood, only carve it off!

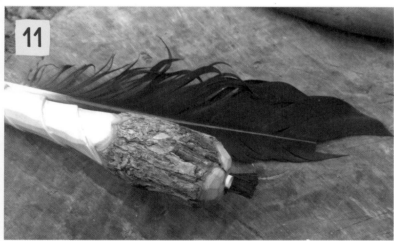

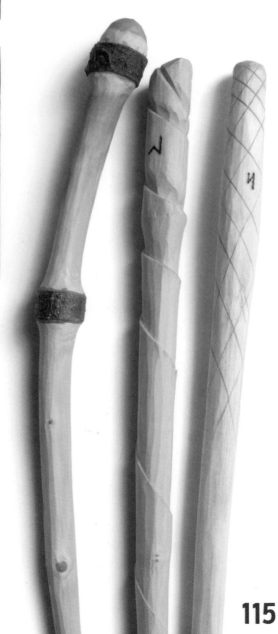

11. Add the magic. Find a feather, hair of a human, animal or mythical beast, and push it into the core at the handle end. You could also add a tiny roll of paper with a magic spell. Then plug the hole with a tightly fitting piece of wood and carve it flush with the end.

Allow the wand to dry for a couple of weeks and then add a coat of oil to protect it from the elements (see page 155). For additional ideas on how to embellish your magic wand see page 156. Remember to always use your wand for good!

It might seem odd to take a large tree, cut it up and make it into smaller, cartoon trees but that is what this project is all about. These tiny trees are a good way to practise small, very controlled, concave cuts (see page 33). They are a smaller, more structured variation on the Fairytale Fungi (see page 86). The trees can be used as story props with the little Stick People (see page 120), they can be threaded and hung up as Christmas decorations or be part of a table centrepiece.

Tiny pine trees

YOU WILL NEED:

- A straight, knot-free length of wood, such as hazel, willow or sycamore, about 20in (50cm) long and ½–1in (1–2cm) in diameter is ideal to start with

- Saw

- Sharp knife

- Acrylic paints

1. Point the top 1–1½in (3–4cm) of the stick either by carving freehand or using a knee pull cut (see page 33).

2. Mark the line between the pine tree branches and trunk just under the point with a vertical stop cut (see page 34) all the way round the stick.

3. Mark the trunk by carving concave cuts (see page 33) towards the stop cut. Repeat the process of making a vertical stop cut and carving towards it to chop away until the trunk is the desired shape. It's a good idea to leave the trunk slightly thicker than the finished shape to give it enough strength to cope with the next stages.

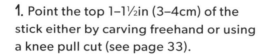

4. Mark three sections of branches with two equally spaced vertical stop cuts. Take care to make the ends of the cuts meet their start point.

5. Define each layer of branches by making small concave cuts from the base to the stop cut. Avoid using the blade as a lever to lift shavings out at the end of the cut, as this can easily lift a chunk of wood from the next layer. If the shavings are not just falling off, then repeat the vertical cut to release them.

6. Repeat for the next whorl of branches and finish the top of the tree with another round of concave cuts up to the point of the tree.

7. Saw the tree from the stick, leaving about ½in (1cm) of bark as a base. Allow the wood to dry indoors for a couple of days and then paint with acrylic or milk paints if desired.

These little characters really fit the description of 'wood doodles' and each one is unique. They are a great prop for imaginative play or they can be combined with story dice to give ideas and structure to the stories that they feature in. The potential variations are endless, and this project can be simplified for younger whittlers by just making a pointed hat and then painting on the detail, or extended by reducing the size of the figures and adding more relief detail. The instructions are for a Norman knight but as you make more, you will be able to adapt the techniques to create your own characters.

Stick people

YOU WILL NEED:

- *A straight, knot-free length of wood, such as hazel, willow or sycamore, about 20in (50cm) long and ½–¾in (1–2cm) in diameter is ideal to start with*
- *Sharp knife*
- *Saw*
- *Pencil*

1. Shape the end of the stick to a dome in several stages. First, taper the end ½in (1.5cm) of the stick, but not to a sharp point. Change the angle of the blade and make the very end of the stick a dull point. Carve away wood from the transition between the first two angles to create a third facet and more of a dome shape. Alternatively, you can roll your wrist away from you while carving to create a more rounded dome.

2. Mark the neck by making a vertical stop cut all the way around the stick.

3. Remove the bark from this cut to the domed end of the stick. You may need to cut towards the line and therefore towards your body (see page 36) to make this a neat line.

4. Mark the rim of the knight's helmet by making a vertical cut almost all the way around the stick. Leave a gap for the nose guard.

5. It may be helpful to use a pencil to mark the shape of the nose guard before making these fiddly little cuts. Make two parallel cuts at right angles to the rim to form the sides of the nose. Use the very tip of the knife to make a vertical cut at the base of the nose. Turn the stick around and repeat this cut in the other direction to make it an even depth right across.

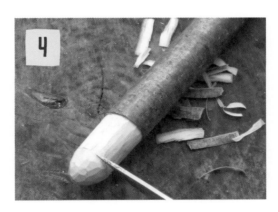

6. Carve all the way around the stick from the neckline to the helmet rim. Use a thumb push cut (see page 35) for fine control at the edge of the helmet. Take special care around the nose and eyes, using the very tip of the knife to follow the vertical cuts made in step 5. It will be easiest to define the side of the head on the same side as the hand holding the knife. To carve the other side will probably require you to turn the wood through 180 degrees and carefully cut towards yourself. To maximize control when making very small and precise cuts, you can choke up the blade by holding it between thumb and forefinger with only about ¼in (0.5cm) of the tip visible. The knife handle should be braced against the heel of the hand.

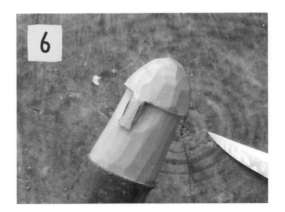

7. A simple mouth can be carved using a triangular chip cut. Press the tip of the knife into the wood where you want the mouth to be to make an incision at about 60 degrees to the surface. Make a second incision at 60 degrees in the other direction with the cuts meeting in a valley under the surface of the wood. Use the tip of the knife to cut from the base of the triangle shape towards the point. This will remove a chip and make an expressive mouth shape.

8. Saw the head from the stick, leaving about ½in (1cm) of bark as a base.

Creating a smooth surface without using sandpaper

Every time you carve away wood with a knife you leave a flat surface or facet. These can be used as an attractive design feature: as the light catches each facet differently, it's clear that the object was made using hand tools rather than a machine. Where two facets meet there will be an angle. But if you want a surface to appear smooth or rounded, then you just need to keep carving smaller and smaller shavings until you have hundreds of barely distinguishable tiny facets and the work will appear and feel quite smooth.

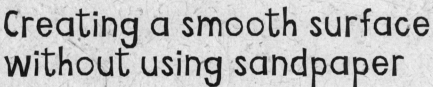

Spanbaum

This little tree is a rustic, greenwood version of the *Spanbaum* (wood-shaving tree) – a traditional German Christmas decoration. It is a satisfying seasonal wood doodle, which develops control and accuracy by making small push cuts with the tip of the knife. It is also a good way of upcycling the spikes of wood left over after the carving of Gypsy Flowers (see page 132). Experiment with wood at different stages in the drying process. You will notice that freshly cut wood produces different types of shavings from drier, more seasoned wood. I prefer to cut willow, sycamore or hazel, peel the bark off and let it dry for a couple of weeks before making these.

YOU WILL NEED:

- *A straight piece of knot-free hardwood, at least 12in (30cm) long and about 1in–1½in (2–3cm) in diameter*
- *Pruning saw or hacksaw*
- *Sharp knife*

1. Use a knee pull cut (see page 33) to point the top 3–4in (8–10cm) of your stick in an even taper.

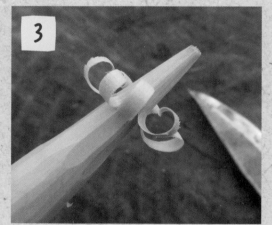

2. Place the knife about 1½in (4cm) from the point of the stick, which will be the top of our tree. Use a thumb push cut (see page 35) to make a ¾in (2cm) long shaving, which will remain attached to the stick. The actual length of this shaving will be determined by how far your pushing thumb will flex before it is straightened and stops exerting any more force on the knife.

3. Repeat this process systematically around the stick until you have completed a whorl of branches. I'm right-handed and always rotate the work clockwise. Try both directions and see which works best for you. Using the tip of the knife to complete each curl reduces the likelihood of chopping off previous curls. Don't worry if you lose a few shavings, you can always try another one in the same place.

4. Move about ¾in (2cm) down the stick and repeat previous steps to make several more whorls below the first. You can experiment with design by making the length of the curls vary as you complete more whorls. If you are finding it difficult to avoid cutting off previous curls, then try carving a single line of shavings in a spiral all the way down the stick.

5. Extend any tight curls into longer branches using a tiny stick to gently unfurl them.

6. Saw the shaving tree from the branch. Leaving some bark on the 'trunk' is a good effect and shows the origin of the wood from which the tree was made.

The Spanbaum, a traditional Christmas decoration, originates in the Ore Mountains in eastern Germany where they are carved from seasoned lime wood and made on a lathe with a chisel.

Making curls

The cut in this example is a slice where the knife draws across the wood and slices through the fibres of the wood rather than pushing them forward like a chisel. This can be seen if you closely observe the part of the blade in contact with the wood as you carve. If you're using a knife in the same way as you would a chisel or woodworking plane, the same part of the blade will be in contact with the wood all the way along the cut. In a slicing motion, you can use the whole length of the blade in a single cut. Changing the angle in which you present the knife to the wood will change the way that the wood curls.

These artificial flowers make a great addition to fresh flower arrangements or make a stylish, everlasting display in a vase of their own. They can be dyed in a jug of diluted food colouring or left in the colour of the wood, which may slowly mellow over time.

As the name suggests, Gypsy Flowers were traditionally made and sold door to door by gypsies and travellers. They would have used young elder branches and inserted the stem into the elder pith. Elder is not my first choice of wood for this project, as it can become quite brittle and harder to work with when it has dried out a little. I use either hazel or willow. Freshly cut, wet wood won't curl and will be more difficult to work with, so I like to let it dry out for a few weeks before use. If I can get hold of overgrown willow, particularly the variety *Salix viminalis*, which is used in living willow structures, then I will often peel it and speed dry it in the car or greenhouse for a couple of days until it becomes ready to use.

Gypsy flowers

YOU WILL NEED:

- *A straight, dry hardwood stick (willow, hazel or sycamore work well), about 20in (50cm) long and ¾–1in (2–3cm) in diameter*

- *A thin, straight stick for the stem – one end should have a diameter the same as your drill bit.*

- *Sharp knife*

- *Pruning saw*

- *Drill with 5mm bit*

1. Peel the bark from the top 8in (20cm) of your main stem stick. This is not essential and the bark can be utilized to make an interesting effect on the first round of petals. However, this is tricky and best left until you have mastered the basic technique and can control the pattern and curl of your petals.

2. Round off the corners with the knife, using the 'apple peeling' cut (see page 37).

3. Drill a ¼in (5mm) hole in the end of the thinner stem stick. This will form the stem of the flower. Making this hole once the flower has been carved is not usually possible, so don't forget this step!

4. Use a knee pull cut (see page 33) to even out any small bumps along the length. Concentrate on feeling the knife bevel in contact with the wood and vary the angle and pressure to take off more or less wood as required.

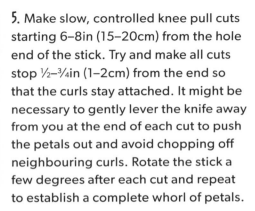

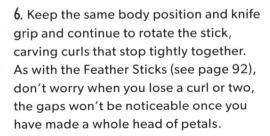

5. Make slow, controlled knee pull cuts starting 6–8in (15–20cm) from the hole end of the stick. Try and make all cuts stop ½–¾in (1–2cm) from the end so that the curls stay attached. It might be necessary to gently lever the knife away from you at the end of each cut to push the petals out and avoid chopping off neighbouring curls. Rotate the stick a few degrees after each cut and repeat to establish a complete whorl of petals.

6. Keep the same body position and knife grip and continue to rotate the stick, carving curls that stop tightly together. As with the Feather Sticks (see page 92), don't worry when you lose a curl or two, the gaps won't be noticeable once you have made a whole head of petals.

7. As the stick thins, make the last few rounds of petals much shorter and the angle of the cuts more acute to eventually free the flower head from the stick.

8. Turn the flower head over, hold it carefully and insert the thick end of your stem stick into the hole drilled in step 3. Cut the stem to length and display.

Rhythm sticks

This deceptively simple instrument incorporates several techniques and requires a fair amount of accuracy, especially in drilling holes and splitting the sides from the body of the instrument. The rhythm sticks are played by shaking them rhythmically and adding extra beats by hitting them on your hand or knee, much like the traditional folk accompaniment of playing the spoons. I was inspired to make this by seeing the children of Lesna Droga Forest Kindergarten in Warsaw making their own from pre-cut and drilled wood.

1. Start with a longer piece of wood than you need for the finished item so that it can be held securely when sawing. Measure about 6in (15cm) from the end of the branch and make a stop cut (see page 34) by sawing about one third of the way through. Turn the wood 180 degrees and make another sawcut one third of the way through, directly opposite the first cut.

2. Measure another 4–5in (10–12cm) along the branch from the stop cuts and saw all the way through to release the work piece.

3. Stand the length of wood cut in step 2 upright on a flat surface. Place the knife on the top and align it with the saw cuts so you can cleave away a section from the side of the branch down to the stop cut.

4. Twist the branch round 180 degrees and cleave away a section from the other side, parallel to the first. The sections you have removed can be discarded.

5. Tidy up the handle by carving flat along the surface so that the stop cuts are no longer visible.

6. Drill two adjacent holes through the whole width of the branch, about ½in (1cm) from the stop cut and perpendicular to the flat of the handle.

7. Carve off all the outer and inner bark from the handle and body of the instrument.

8. Carefully line up the knife to cleave away the sides of the branch from the body of the instrument. It's possible that the side section will 'run off' towards the edge of the branch. Go slowly! If it looks like this might happen then it's possible to turn the wood around and baton (see page 34) from the other end towards the stop cut. Don't worry if the split does not work as you intended. Every piece of wood is different and with experience you may be able to predict how a split will run. Sometimes it's just a matter of thinking laterally and adapting the thing you're making to the way the wood behaves.

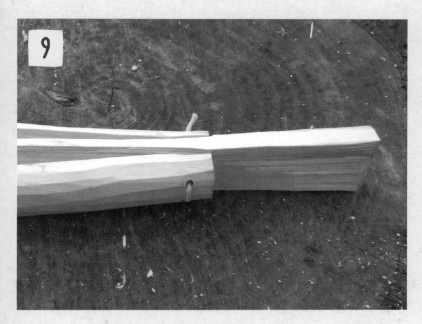

9. Reattach the two slices to the handle by threading a length of string through the holes and tying it tightly with a reef or overhand knot.

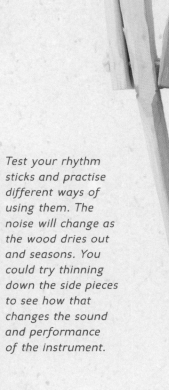

Test your rhythm sticks and practise different ways of using them. The noise will change as the wood dries out and seasons. You could try thinning down the side pieces to see how that changes the sound and performance of the instrument.

This quotation from Nicholas Culpeper, written in the 17th century, gives us a little insight into the life of a British child of the time. Having to make your own toys from the plants around you meant that you would have had knowledge of what to use and the tools (knife) and skills to make your own when you wanted to. Everyone who had made a pop-gun knew what elder wood looked like, so Culpeper didn't waste any ink describing it in his book.

There are plenty of variations on the design of the pop-gun or spud gun. The version below is fairly simple and uses a piece of potato to create a seal at the end of the plunger. Like many hedgerow toys, it may just last a day and then stop working and be discarded, but the making is part of the fun.

Elder spud gun

YOU WILL NEED:

- *A length of elder stem about 8–12in (20–30cm) long and ½–1½in (2–4cm) in diameter. The section should have a leaf or branch node at one end. It's important that the pith is wider than your tent peg and ideally ¼in (6mm) or bigger*
- *A straight, dry length of willow or hazel with a diameter just smaller than the pith of the elder*
- *A long wire tent peg*
- *Sharp knife*
- *Pruning saw*
- *Potato (raw)*

1. Measure just under one tent peg's length from the end of the stick and saw off the node section. Keep this, as it will become the handle of the plunger.

2. Push the pith out of the long section to make a tube. Use the end and side of the tent peg to scrape and burnish the inner wall of the tube to make it as smooth as possible.

3. Push a small-diameter stick into the pith of the short section that was sawn off in step 1. The pith often constricts at the nodes and will probably stop the thin stick from poking all the way through the plunger handle. Check that the plunger will slide smoothly through the elder tube, then cut it to length slightly shorter than the length of the tube.

4. Use the knife to sharpen the end of the pop-gun like a pencil. This will need to have a sharp enough edge all the way round to be able to cut through a slice of raw potato.

5. Cut a ½in (1cm) slice of uncooked potato then push the sharpened nozzle of the pop-gun in it to cut a plug, which will stay in the barrel of the gun.

6. Use the plunger to ram the potato plug at least halfway down the barrel.

7. Cut another potato plug as in step 5. Leave this one as it is, in the nozzle of the gun.

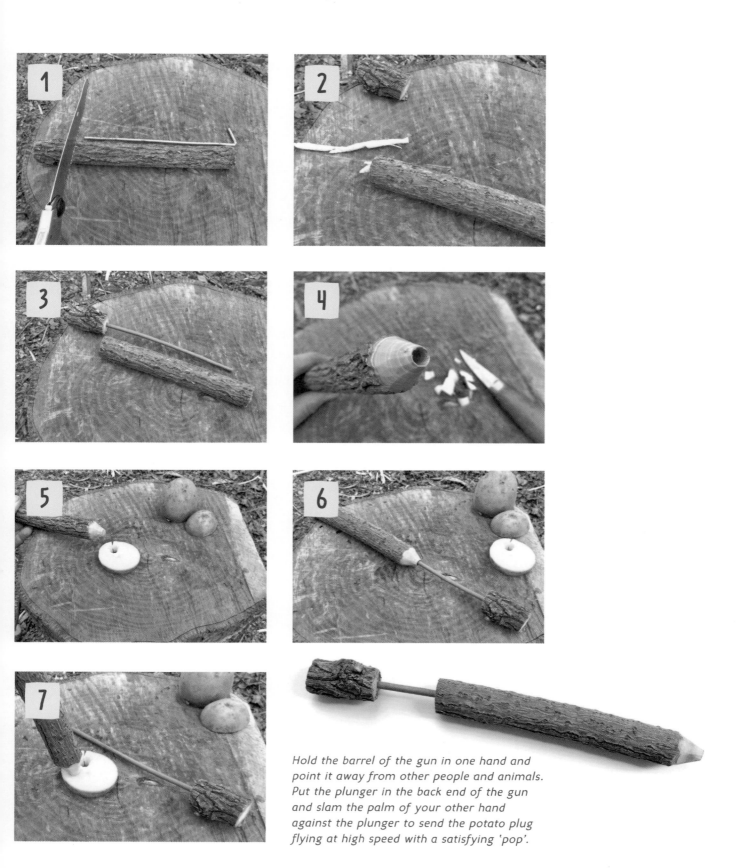

Hold the barrel of the gun in one hand and point it away from other people and animals. Put the plunger in the back end of the gun and slam the palm of your other hand against the plunger to send the potato plug flying at high speed with a satisfying 'pop'.

This dart gun involves more advanced woodcrafting skills, and should only be attempted when you are comfortable with all of the techniques in the preceding projects. Younger children should definitely have adult supervision.

The idea for it came from an obscure Breton film, which showed an old folk museum in Brittany with a large collection of traditional children's folk toys. The only other reference for the toy that I could find was in *The American Boy's Handy Book* by Daniel Carter Beard, published in 1882, where whalebone is suggested as a spring!

There's lots of fun to be had in tweaking this to increase the range of the gun by lengthening the slot and using different materials for the spring.

Dart gun

YOU WILL NEED:

- *A straight elder branch, about 20in (50cm) long and 1–1½in (3–4cm) in diameter. Try to include as few nodes as possible and make sure that the pith is bigger than ¼in (4mm)*

- *A straight, thin, freshly cut hazel or willow 'whip' about 5ft (1.5m) long and at least ¼in (5mm) in diameter*

- *A thin, straight stick, 12–15in (30–40cm) long, which has a smaller diameter than the pith of the elder*

- *Sharp knife*

- *A long tent peg, stiff fencing wire or metal coat hanger*

- *Pruning saw*

- *Drill with a 5mm bit*

- *Pencil or marker pen*

1. Poke the pith into the elder up to about 8in (20cm) deep. Smooth the bore so that no pith is left attached to the sides of the tube. If using wire or a coat hanger, use an offcut of elder to make a handle.

2. Peel the bark by hand if you wish to. It will be easier to mark out the firing channel on bare wood.

3. Use a pencil or marker pen to mark out a long rectangle on the stem. It should be as wide as the pith diameter and about 5–6in (12–15cm) long.

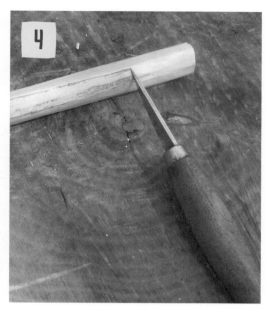

4. Make vertical stop cuts (see page 34) on the short edges of the rectangle.

5. Carve a 'V'-shaped channel between the stop cuts, along the middle of the rectangle. Either draw the knife carefully towards you, as described on page 36, or use a series of short thumb push cuts (see page 35) away from you to maintain control.

6. Enlarge this channel until all wood has been removed from the shaded area and you have made a rectangular window through to the bore of the tube.

7. Turn the wood over and carefully mark out another rectangle directly opposite the first. Repeat steps 4 to 6 on this side until you have made a window all the way through the stick.

8. Cut a hazel 'whip' from dense growth, where it is tall, straight and without side branches. It would be about 5ft (1.5m) long and ¼–½in (0.5–1cm) in diameter at the base. Remove any leaves or bud scars and measure it up for size.

9. Drill a ¼in (5mm) hole all the way through the stick, in line with the carved window at the back end of the dart gun. You may need to clean up or enlarge the hole with the tip of your knife.

10. Insert the thin end of the hazel whip through the bottom of the hole and push through until it fits tightly. Gently bend the whip over and bring the thin end down through the window. The bark may shed as it is pushed through the hole, but this is not a problem. The protruding thick end of the branch makes a good handle or grip.

11. Make an 8–12in (20–30cm) long, straight dart from a small-diameter straight branch, plant-support stick or bamboo skewer. Insert it into the barrel of the dart gun, (thin end first) until about an inch (a couple of centimetres) of it are visible in the window. Pull back the hazel whip spring and release. The spring will move forward, hit the end of the dart and shoot it from the barrel. Experiment with different types and lengths of darts and ways of loading them until you discover the optimal projectile launch.

Finishing and decorating

Wood is often beautiful enough to need very little adornment apart from a coat of oil that can really bring the grain and 'figure' of the wood to life. Additional patterns can be made by chip carving (see page 156), or they can be 'tattooed' onto the wood by a technique called kolrosing (see page 156). Sometimes it can be fun to add colour to wood by using earth pigments (see below) or bright paints, or wrap it with wool, plant fibres, feathers and other found objects. It's fun to experiment and try things out.

I no longer use sandpaper on anything I make. I found the process of sanding tedious; the dust it creates meant that I needed to wear a mask, and sometimes it felt as though I was just taking a big eraser to hide my mistakes. There's no shame in using abrasives to smooth your work but as your tool sharpening and carving skills improve, it will become much easier to do without them. A finish that shows tool marks demonstrates the skill of the carver and distinguishes what you've made from machine produced items. The following information will help you to get started on the exciting journey of embellishment.

Oil

There is a wide range of oils available for use on wood. If you are oiling any object to be used with food or which might end up in a child's mouth, then you'll need to use a food-safe oil which will go hard over time without solvents or additives. Walnut oil and flaxseed oil (raw, not boiled), also known as linseed oil, both work well but will take some time to harden or 'go off'. Tung oil and Danish oil will set more rapidly and are easily available in hardware stores. Do not use cooking oils like sunflower or olive oils, as they will become rancid and sticky rather than harden.

Earth pigment

It's fun to make the natural colours of your neighbourhood into paint by finding different tones in the soil as you dig to different depths in one place or travel around an area. Classic colours like burnt sienna and red ochre can be purchased from art suppliers. But soil, clay, charcoal and softer rocks can be sieved and ground up into fine dust in a mortar and pestle. When they are mixed with a binding agent such as oil, egg or milk, they can make beautiful and long-lasting natural paints. Make sure to wear eye protection and gloves if breaking rocks.

Apply the paint to your work with a normal paintbrush, rag, your fingers or experiment with natural brushes such as a feather or a clump of dried up moss.

I sometimes make milk paint to use on wood and have found Steve Tomlin's recipe (see page 158) as follows, to be easy and reliable: mix 4 parts milk powder, 1 part bicarbonate of soda, 1 part pigment, 6 parts cold water and let sit for an hour before using.

Alternatively, the pigments can be added directly to linseed oil, egg yolks or an emulsion of both. It's also worth spending time researching old recipes and trying them out on your work.

IT CAN BE FUN TO GRIND BRIGHTLY COLOURED PETALS IN THE SPRING OR FRUITS LIKE HAWS AND BLACKBERRIES IN THE AUTUMN. THE COLOURS RELEASED ARE NOT ALWAYS AS YOU MIGHT IMAGINE AND, UNLIKE EARTH PIGMENTS, MANY WILL FADE TO GREY OR LIGHT BROWN IN A SHORT PERIOD OF TIME.

Pens and paints

A permanent black marker pen is good to have in your pocket for adding little details such as the eyes and a nose to our foxes. If working with a group of children this will also be invaluable for naming work. The consequences of children's creations getting mixed up can be traumatic! Simple, spontaneous colouring can be done with ordinary felt-tipped pens but brighter effects can be achieved with acrylic paints. Some people consider the colours garish or plastic paints incongruous for use with natural wood. However, I think they add a great deal of character to tiny mushrooms and little people. Most importantly, children like painting their work with them.

Fur, fibre and feathers

Most children I work with outdoors, enjoy collecting things like feathers, shells, stones, bones, sticks and cones. These intrinsically important objects can be used to enhance and adorn many projects by lashing and tying with wool or other natural fibres.

Kolrosing

Pronounced 'coal-rose-ing', this technique involves scoring a pattern, drawing or lettering into the surface of the wood with a thin, sharp blade then rubbing finely ground powder such as instant coffee, cinnamon or charcoal into the cuts before oiling and burnishing the wood. An excellent guide to the process is available in a free eBook by Ty Thornock (see page 158).

Chip carving

There are many books and specialist sets of tools dedicated to this area of woodworking. For our purposes, small chips of wood can be removed from an edge or flat surface to make a three-dimensional geometric pattern, such as a zigzag. The tip of a Sloyd knife (see page 19) is perfect for making vertical incisions (tiny stop cuts) and removing the wood between them with a tiny horizontal slice. I especially like this scale pattern for fish and dragons.

Thanks to:

Suzie, Jake and Stan, for testing ideas, commenting on drafts, photography and keeping me going; Alan Bruford, for the inspiration of the strange artefacts that litter his desk, especially the Little Pots (p.48); Marion Hedtke, who was as excited as I was by her discovery of the Duck Caller (p.60); Lily Horseman, for first posting a picture of the Skulk of Foxes (p.98) on social media; Dave Jackson, who eventually showed me the trick behind a Whimmy Diddle (p.70); Janig and Morwena Stephens, for the Breton Toy Museum DVD where I first saw the Elder Dart Gun (p.146); Stan, who invented so many new Stick People characters (p.120); Sean Hellman, for the strop (p.41) that changed my life; Hector Christie and Daphne at Tapeley Park; Dominique Page, Commissioning and Senior Project Editor at GMC Publications, for inviting me to write and expertly guiding the whole process; all of the European Institute for Outdoor Adventure Education and Experiential Learning tribe; and the UK Forest School community, especially the Forest School Association South West Group, who so freely share ideas and push the movement forwards.

Resources

Forest Education
Forest Education Network
www.lotc.org.uk/fen

Forest School Association
www.forestschoolassociation.org

Irish Forest School association
www.irishforestschoolassociation.ie

Outdoor and Woodland Learning Scotland (OWLS)
www.owlscotland.org

Outdoor Learning Wales (OLW)
www.outdoorlearningwales.org

Trees and Woodlands
Forestry England
www.forestryengland.uk/discover

International Tree Foundation
www.internationaltreefoundation.org

Royal Forestry Society
www.rfs.org.uk

Small Woods Association
www.smallwoods.org.uk

Sylva Foundation
www.sylva.org.uk

Woodland Trust
www.woodlandtrust.org.uk/trees-woods-and-wildlife/british-trees

Knife Law
www.gov.uk/buying-carrying-knives

Tools and Equipment
Axminster
Extensive range of tools and machinery
www.axminster.co.uk

Muddy Faces
Everything Forest School and outdoor learning
www.muddyfaces.co.uk

Nordic Outdoor
For a good range of Mora knives and Scandinavian outdoor gear
www.nordicoutdoor.co.uk

Woodcraft Supply LLC
For a variety of carving and whittling hand tools
www.woodcraft.com

Woodsmiths Store
All sorts of specialist and harder to find items for greenwood work and traditional woodland crafts
https://woodsmithexperience.co.uk

Blacksmiths
British Artist Blacksmiths Association
www.babamembers.org.uk

The Artist-Blacksmith's Association of North America, Inc
https://abana.org

Worshipful Company of Blacksmiths
https://blacksmithscompany.co.uk/craft/find-a-smith

Finishing
UK artist Pete Ward uses earth pigments and has produced the following guide for teachers: https://intim8ecology.files.wordpress.com/2011/04/earth-pigments-in-north-devon-a-teachers-guide-2.pdf

For milk paint recipe (see Finishing and Decorating, page 155): https://stevetomlincrafts.wordpress.com/2013/01/23/milk-paint-recipe

For Kolrosing, see the free pdf of *Kolrosing spoons – an illustrated guide* by Ty Thornock: www.wrigley.me.uk/stuff/spoons/kolrosing-A5-FINAL-small.pdf

Sharpening
Having personal experience of their advice and products, I would recommend Sean Hellman, Robin Wood and Ben Orford. Search for videos on YouTube with any of these names and key in 'sharpening' for expert, tried and tested advice on sharpening knives and axes.

Books
Swedish Carving Techniques by Wille Sundqvist (Taunton, 2013)

The Teacher's Hand-Book Of Slöjd by Otto Salomon (Forgotten Books, 2018)

Woodland Craft by Ben Law (GMC Publications, 2015)

Index

To order a book contact: GMC Publications Ltd, Castle Place, 166 High Street, Lewes, East Sussex, BN7 1XU, United Kingdom
Tel: +44 (0)1273 488005. www.gmcbooks.com